Eyewitness
WEATHER

19th-century
angle barometer

Weather on
the plains

Mountain weather

19th-century
aneroid
barometer

Early Florentine
mercury
barometer and
thermometer

Model of mountain
weather patterns

Macrophotograph of a snow crystal

Eyewitness
WEATHER

Written by
BRIAN COSGROVE

Pocket hygrometer

Weather cock

Early English thermometer

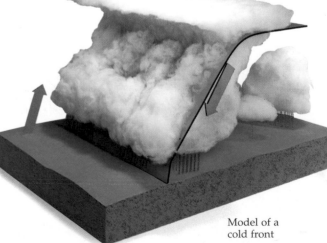

Model of a cold front

DK

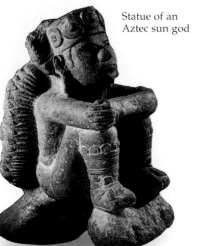

Statue of an
Aztec sun god

Open and shut pinecones, indicating
damp or dry weather

Quadrant

DK

LONDON, NEW YORK,
MELBOURNE, MUNICH, and DELHI

Project editors John Farndon, Marion Dent
Art editor Alison Anholt-White
Senior editor Helen Parker
Senior art editors Jacquie Gulliver, Julia Harris
Production Louise Barratt
Picture research Diana Morris
Special photography Karl Shone, Keith Percival
Editorial consultant Jim Sharp

PAPERBACK EDITION
Managing editors Andrew Macintyre, Camilla Hallinan
Managing art editors Jane Thomas, Martin Wilson
Publishing manager Sunita Gahir
Category publisher Andrea Pinnington
Editors Angela Wilkes, Sue Nicholson
Art editor Catherine Goldsmith
Production Jenny Jacoby, Georgina Hayworth
Picture research Sarah Pownall, Kate Lockley
DTP designer Siu Chan, Andy Hilliard, Ronaldo Julien

This Eyewitness ® Guide has been conceived by
Dorling Kindersley Limited and Editions Gallimard

First published in Great Britain in 1991
Revised edition published in 2007 by
Dorling Kindersley Limited,
80 Strand, London WC2R ORL

This edition produced in 2008 for The Book People,
Hall Wood Avenue, Haydock, St. Helen's, WA11 9UL

A CIP catalogue record for this book is
available from the British Library.

ISBN 978-1-40533-105-0

Colour reproduction by Colourscan, Singapore
Printed in China by Toppan Printing Co., (Shenzhen) Ltd.

Early Florentine
glass thermometer

A Fitzroy
barometer

Discover more at
www.dk.com

Contents

Orrery from the 18th century showing the motion of the planets and the seasons

The restless air

OUR PLANET IS SURROUNDED by a blanket of gases called the atmosphere. If it were not for the atmosphere we would not be able to live – we would be burned by the intense heat of the sun in the day or frozen by the icy chill of night. Look into the sky on a clear day, and you can see the atmosphere stretching some 1,000 km (600 miles) above you. Perhaps 99 per cent of it is as calm and unchanging as space beyond. But the very lowest 10 km (6 miles) – the air in which we live and breathe – is forever on the move, boiling and bubbling in the sun's heat like a vast cauldron on a fire. It is the constant swirling and stirring of this lowest layer of the atmosphere, called the troposphere, which gives us everything we call weather, from the warm, still days of summer to the wildest storms of winter.

TAKING THE AIR
James Glaisher and Robert Coxwell were just two of many brave researchers who, in the 19th century, risked their lives in balloons to find out about the atmosphere. They found that the air got colder the higher they went. By 1902, though, unmanned balloons proved it got colder with height only up to a certain point called the tropopause, or the top of the troposphere.

Bank of cloud along the equator, marking the zone where the north and south trade winds meet

Whirls of cloud show the depressions that bring much bad weather to the mid-latitudes (pp. 32–35)

Belt of rain swept in by a depression

Dry, clear air over the Sahara desert

Clouds aligned with the steady northeasterly trade winds blowing towards the equator

Europe

Africa

BREATH FOR LIFE
The nature of air intrigued scientists for centuries. Then in the 1770s, Joseph Priestley's experiments with mice showed that air contains something that animals need to live. Like many, he thought this was a substance called phlogiston.

PLANET OF CLOUDS
In photographs from space, great swirls of cloud can be seen enveloping the Earth. These swirls dramatically highlight the constant motion of gases in the troposphere that gives us all our weather. Many of the world's major weather patterns can be seen clearly. Along the equator, for instance, is a ribbon of cloud thousands of kilometres long, formed because the intense heat of the sun here stirs up strong updraughts. These carry moisture from the ocean so high into the air that it cools and condenses to form clouds (pp. 24-25).

Whirls of cloud around mid-latitude depressions

Atlantic Ocean

Zone where unpredictable westerly winds blow

WHAT IS AIR?
In the 1780s, French chemist Antoine Lavoisier found that Priestley's vital something was a gas, which he called oxygen. He also found that air contained two other gases – nitrogen and carbon dioxide. Later, air was found to be roughly 21% oxygen, 78% nitrogen, and less than 1% carbon dioxide and other gases.

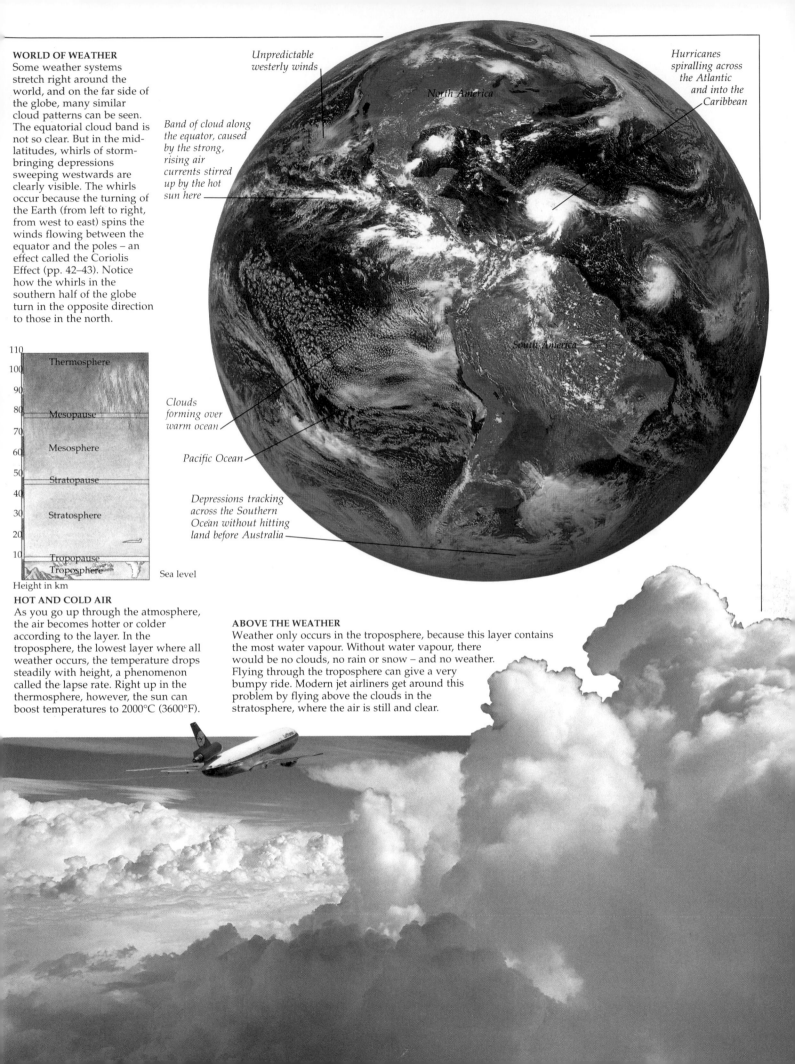

WORLD OF WEATHER

Some weather systems stretch right around the world, and on the far side of the globe, many similar cloud patterns can be seen. The equatorial cloud band is not so clear. But in the mid-latitudes, whirls of storm-bringing depressions sweeping westwards are clearly visible. The whirls occur because the turning of the Earth (from left to right, from west to east) spins the winds flowing between the equator and the poles – an effect called the Coriolis Effect (pp. 42–43). Notice how the whirls in the southern half of the globe turn in the opposite direction to those in the north.

Unpredictable westerly winds

North America

Hurricanes spiralling across the Atlantic and into the Caribbean

Band of cloud along the equator, caused by the strong, rising air currents stirred up by the hot sun here

South America

Clouds forming over warm ocean

Pacific Ocean

Depressions tracking across the Southern Ocean without hitting land before Australia

110
100 — Thermosphere
90
80 — Mesopause
70
60 — Mesosphere
50 — Stratopause
40
30 — Stratosphere
20
10 — Tropopause
Troposphere — Sea level
Height in km

HOT AND COLD AIR

As you go up through the atmosphere, the air becomes hotter or colder according to the layer. In the troposphere, the lowest layer where all weather occurs, the temperature drops steadily with height, a phenomenon called the lapse rate. Right up in the thermosphere, however, the sun can boost temperatures to 2000°C (3600°F).

ABOVE THE WEATHER

Weather only occurs in the troposphere, because this layer contains the most water vapour. Without water vapour, there would be no clouds, no rain or snow – and no weather. Flying through the troposphere can give a very bumpy ride. Modern jet airliners get around this problem by flying above the clouds in the stratosphere, where the air is still and clear.

Natural signs

SAILORS, FARMERS, AND OTHERS whose livelihood depends on the weather learned long ago that the world around them gave all kinds of clues to the weather to come – as long as they knew what to look for. Age-old advice passed down from generation to generation is offered on anything from the colour of the sky to the feel of your boots in the morning. Of course, some country weather lore is little more than superstition and all but useless for weather forecasting. But much is based on close observation of the natural world and can give an accurate prediction of the weather. Tiny variations in the air, which we cannot feel, often affect plants and animals. A change in their appearance or behaviour can be the sign of a change in the weather.

WHAT'S THE WEATHER LIKE?
Everyone – from travellers to sailors – had to know about the weather and be aware of natural signs around them.

NOTHING BUT A GROUNDHOG *above*
In the USA, 2 February is Groundhog Day. People say that if you can see a groundhog's shadow at noon on this day, the weather will be cold for six weeks. Sadly, weather records have proved the groundhog wrong many times.

SUN DAY OPENING
The scarlet pimpernel is often known as the "poor man's weather glass". Its tiny flowers open wide in sunny weather, but close up tightly when rain is in the air.

Sunset

Sunrise

SEEING RED
Old country wisdom says, *Red sky at night, Shepherds' delight; Red sky in the morning, Shepherds' warning* – which means a fiery sunset should be followed by a fine morning, and a fiery dawn by storms. This is one folk saying that is often true.

WEATHER WEED
People near the sea often hang out strands of kelp, for seaweed is one of the best natural weather forecasters. In fine weather, the kelp shrivels and is dry to the touch. If rain (pp. 30–31) threatens, the weed swells and feels damp.

CURLY WARNING
Wool is very responsive to the humidity, or moistness, of the air. When the air is dry, it shrinks and curls up. If rain is on its way, the air is moist, and the wool swells and straightens out.

Wet   Dry

WEATHER CONES
A pine cone is one of the most reliable of all natural weather indicators. In dry weather, the scales on a pine cone open out; when they close up, it is a good sign that rain is on the way. This is because, in dry weather, the scales shrivel up and stand out stiffly. When the air is damp, they absorb moisture and become pliable again, allowing the cone to regain its normal shape.

CRICKET FORECAST
Like many small creatures, grasshoppers are sensitive to changes in the weather, chirruping louder and louder as the temperature rises. The chirruping is not actually a song, but the sound of their hind legs rubbing rapidly against their hard front wings.

GLORIOUS MORNING
Like the scarlet pimpernel, the petals of morning glory open and shut in response to weather conditions. These wide-open blooms indicate fine weather.

Oak   Ash

SOAK OR SPLASH?
According to some country weather lore, natural signs can indicate the weather for many days to come, as well as just the next few hours. An old English saying, for instance, is that: *If the oak flowers before the ash, we shall have a splash* (meaning only light rain for the next month or so). *If the ash flowers before the oak, we shall have a soak* (meaning very wet weather). There is little evidence to support any of these long-range predictions.

LYING COWS
When you can see cows lying down in a field, it is sometimes said that rain must be on the way. Apparently, the cows sense the dampness in the air and are making sure they have somewhere dry to lie. While many animals can indeed sense changes in the weather before humans, this particular prediction proves wrong as often as right.

SPRING IS HERE
Many natural signs are said to herald the end of winter, such as the first blooming of the white flowers of the horse chestnut tree. It is true that the flowers will only appear once the weather is mild enough – but this is no guarantee that there will be no more winter storms.

WINTER'S TAIL
Some country folk expect a severe winter if in autumn squirrels have very bushy tails, or gather big stores of nuts. Scientists have found no evidence to support this.

The science of weather

WEATHER AND THE ATMOSPHERE attracted
the attention of thinkers and academics as
long ago as the days of ancient Greece. It was
the Greek philosopher Aristotle who gave us
the word "meteorology" for the scientific
study of weather. In the 17th century, in
Renaissance Italy, the first instruments were
developed to measure changes in the
temperature of the air, its pressure, or
weight, and its moisture content. It was in
Italy, around 1600, that the great astronomer
and mathematician Galileo Galilei made the
first thermometer. Called the thermoscope, it was notoriously
inaccurate. Some 40 years later Galileo's secretary-cum-assistant
Torricelli made the first practical barometer for measuring the
pressure of the air. The first really successful thermometer
was one made by German physicist Daniel Farenheit in
about 1709 using alcohol, followed in 1714 by one
he made using mercury. He also produced
some of the earliest meteorological
instruments for studying
the weather.

HEAT BALLS
Perhaps the first to
prove that air
expands when
heated was Philo, a
philosopher from the
2nd century B.C., who lived in
Byzantium (now Istanbul in
Turkey). When he connected a
pipe from a hollow lead ball
to a jug of water, air bubbled
through the water when the
ball was heated by the sun.

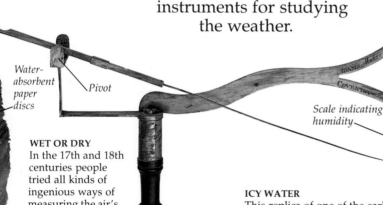

Water-absorbent paper discs

Pivot

Scale indicating humidity

WET OR DRY
In the 17th and 18th
centuries people
tried all kinds of
ingenious ways of
measuring the air's
invisible moisture
content. This simple
hygrometer does just
that. It is an English
instrument dating
from the early 18th
century and consists
of a balance with a pile
of soft paper discs on one arm.
If the air is dry, the discs dry
out and weigh less. If the air is
damp, they absorb water and
weigh more, pulling the
pointer up.

ICY WATER
This replica of one of the earliest, accurate
hygrometers, designed by Grand Duke
Ferdinand II in 1657, has a hollow core
which can be filled with ice. Moisture in the
air condenses on the outside and runs
down into a measuring cylinder. The
amount of water that is collected indicates
the humidity of the air.

Flask for collecting water

GALILEO GALILEI
Galileo
believed that
air has weight,
and asked his assistant Torricelli to solve
why a suction pump will not raise a column
of water higher than about 9 m (30 ft). In
solving this, Torrelli rejected conventional
views and invented the barometer.

WEATHER ACADEMY
The *Accademia del Cimento* in Florence became the focus of early scientific study of the atmosphere. This painting shows members of the academy in 1657, conducting an experiment on heat and cold. Using a thermometer, a mirror, and a bucket of ice, they are trying to find out if cold, like heat, can be reflected. It cannot.

Thermometer

Barometer

Surface of water in tube

Needle indicating air pressure

EARLY WEATHER
The Italian script of this early 18th-century barometer shows how clearly people understood the barometer's value for forecasting weather.

Italian script describing expected weather

CROWN GLASS
Early Florentine meteorologists were served by the most skilled glass blowers in Europe, and it was their skill which made many of the earliest instruments possible. This elaborate and beautiful thermometer dates from shortly after the time of Galileo. Temperatures are registered by the rise and fall of coloured glass balls in the water contained in the tubes.

Balls made of coloured glass

Mercury reservoir

QUICKSILVER TUBE
This is a mercury barometer and thermometer which became available in the early 18th century. Such barometers came into widespread use for measuring air pressure and worked by showing changes in the level of liquid quicksilver, or mercury, in a glass tube open to the air at the base. The level varies because when the air pressure is high, it weighs heavily on the mercury at the base, pushing it farther up the tube. When air pressure is low, the level of mercury drops.

EVANGELISTA TORRICELLI
In 1644, Torricelli made the first barometer, and proved the existence of air pressure. He filled a 1-m (3-ft) glass tube with mercury, then held the open end under the surface in a bowl of mercury. The mercury in the tube dropped to about 80 cm (32 in), leaving a vacuum at the top of the tube. Torricelli realized it was the weight, or pressure, of air on the mercury in the bowl that stopped it falling further.

Paper strip

DIAL HYGROMETER
The needle of this early hygrometer is made to move by a paper strip which shrinks or stretches in response to the dampness of the air.

Watching the weather

MODERN WEATHER FORECASTING
depends on gathering together and
assessing millions of observations
and measurements of atmospheric
conditions, constantly recorded at the same time all over the
world. No single system of measurements can give
meteorologists a complete picture, so information is fed in
from a wide range of sources. Most important are the many,
land-based weather stations, from city centres to remote
islands. Ships and radio signals from drifting weather buoys
report details of conditions at sea. Balloons and specially-
equipped aeroplanes take measurements up through the
atmosphere, while out in space weather satellites constantly
circle the Earth, beaming back pictures of cloud and
temperature patterns.

*Atmospheric
research aircraft*

*Nose of plane
is studded
with an array
of sensors*

*Air
sampler*

*Radio
transmitter
for sending
data via
satellite to
base*

*Temperature and
humidity probes
inside screen*

Navigation light

Anemometer

*Transmitter
aerial*

*Wind vane
for
measuring
wind
direction*

STORM TOSSED
The need for ships to have advance warning
of storms at sea encouraged people to set up
organized weather forecasting networks.

*Barometric
pressure sensor*

*Thermometers in
ventilated white
surround*

*Anemometer for
measuring wind speed*

*Transmitter
gives buoy
position to
orbiting
satellite*

SEA WATCH
Since the 1970s,
drifting weather
buoys have been
used to help fill in
the gaps left by
ship's observations
about conditions at
sea. There are about
such 1,250 buoys,
which float freely
with the ocean
currents and send
readings back to
land via satellites.
The satellites can
pinpoint where the
buoy is to within
2 km (1 mile).

FIXED STATION
At the heart of the world's
weather watching is a
network of about 11,000
permanent weather stations,
linked together by the World
Meteorological Organization.
Most of these stations send
reports every three hours
(called "synoptic hours") to
a number of main weather
centres around the world.
The centres then pass on this
weather data so that different
countries can make up their
own weather forecasts.

*Solar panel to power
navigation light*

HIGH VIEW

Since 1960, satellite pictures have played a vital role in monitoring the weather. They provide two basic types of picture. Normal photographs show the Earth and clouds just as we would see them, while infrared pictures record infrared radiation to show temperatures at the nearest visible point.

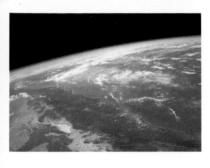

"Blister" on fuselage houses radiation monitoring equipement

Sensors mounted on under-wing pylon

Plane carries a crew of three and up to eighteen scientists

OUT OF THIS WORLD

There are two types of weather satellite. Geostationary satellites always remain fixed in the same spot, usually high above the equator, about 36,000 km (21,600 miles) out in space. There are eight of them altogether, providing an almost complete picture of the globe (except for the two poles) every half hour. Polar-orbiting satellites circle the Earth in strips from pole to pole. They have a lower orbit and provide a changing, more detailed weather picture from closer to the Earth's surface. In 2006, there were about 20 polar-orbiting satellites.

JOSEPH HENRY

In 1848, Joseph Henry of the Smithsonian Institution in the USA, set up a system to obtain simultaneous weather reports from across the continent. By 1849, over 200 observers were taking measurements nation-wide and sending them back to Mr. Henry in Washington. These were displayed on a large map in the Institution, and provided daily weather reports for the Washington Evening Post.

FLYING LABORATORY

Specially-modified research aircraft are fitted with an array of sophisticated equipment to assess weather conditions at various levels in the atmosphere. In the USA, there are even aircraft that are adapted so that they can fly right into the eye of a hurricane. This plane, operated by the UK's Facility for Airborne Atmospheric Measurements, is designed to take a wide range of readings to do with weather and climate, including levels of solar, microwave, and other radiation, and the atmospheric concentrations of ozone and "greenhouse" gases (pp. 60–61) such as carbon dioxide and methane.

Onboard scientist checking data

SKY PROBE

At midnight and midday Greenwich Mean Time, hundreds of helium, gas-filled balloons are launched into the upper atmosphere all around the world. As they rise higher and higher, automatic instruments frequently take humidity, pressure, and temperature readings. These are radioed to the ground and the instrument package is called a radiosonde. Wind speed at various heights can be calculated by tracking the way the balloon rises.

Balloon is tracked either by radar or visually with survey equipment

Tube for filling balloon with helium gas

Long line for supporting recording instruments

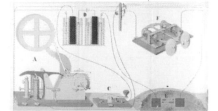

DATA COLLECTION

A crucial advance in accurate weather forecasting was Samuel Morse's invention of the telegraph in the 1840s. Complex messages were sent instantly over long distances through electric cables, by tapping out a coded sequence of short and long pauses, known as the Morse Code. Once a telegraph network was established, weather observations were sent back to a central bureau, giving a complete picture of a continent's weather.

Forecasting

Experienced weather watchers still predict local weather using simple instruments and careful observations of the skies. Larger-scale forecasting – the kind that provides daily radio and television bulletins – is a much more sophisticated and complex process. Every minute of the day and night, weather observations taken by weather stations, ships, satellites, balloons, and radar all around the world are swapped by means of a special Global Telecommunications System, or GTS. At major forecasting centres, all this data is continuously fed into powerful supercomputers, able to carry out millions of calculations a second. Meteorologists use this information to make short-range weather forecasts for the next 24 hours, and draw up a special map, or "synoptic chart", indicating air pressure, wind, cloud cover, temperature, and humidity. Also they can make fairly accurate long-range forecasts for up to a week.

CHANGE OF AIR
French physicist Jean de Borda first showed that changes in air pressure are related to wind speed.

RAIN SCAN
Radar has proved invaluable in monitoring rainfall. Radar signals reflect any rain, hail, or snow within range, and the reflection's intensity shows how heavily rain is falling. Computer calculations then let meteorologists compile a map of rainfall intensity, as above.

HIGH DAYS
Fair weather, with blue skies and fluffy cumulus clouds (pp. 24–25), is often associated with high-pressure zones, or "anticyclones".

Spiked and humped lines indicate occluded fronts, where cold fronts move beneath warm fronts and lift the warm air clear of the ground (pp. 32–35)

Spiked lines indicate a cold front, where cold air is pushing under warm

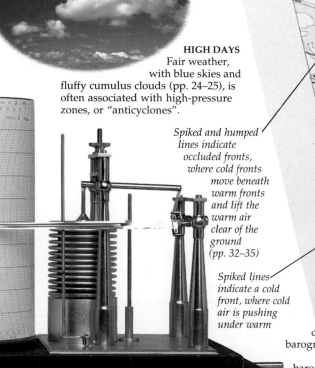

BAROGRAPH
Many fixed weather stations are equipped with a barograph to make a continuous record of changing air pressure. Like most barographs, this one is based around an aneroid barometer. Unlike mercury barometers (pp. 10–11), aneroid barometers have a drum, containing a vacuum sealed at a particular air pressure. As the air pressure changes, the drum expands and contracts. In a barograph, a pen attached to the lid of the drum draws the ups and downs continuously on a rotating sheet of graph paper.

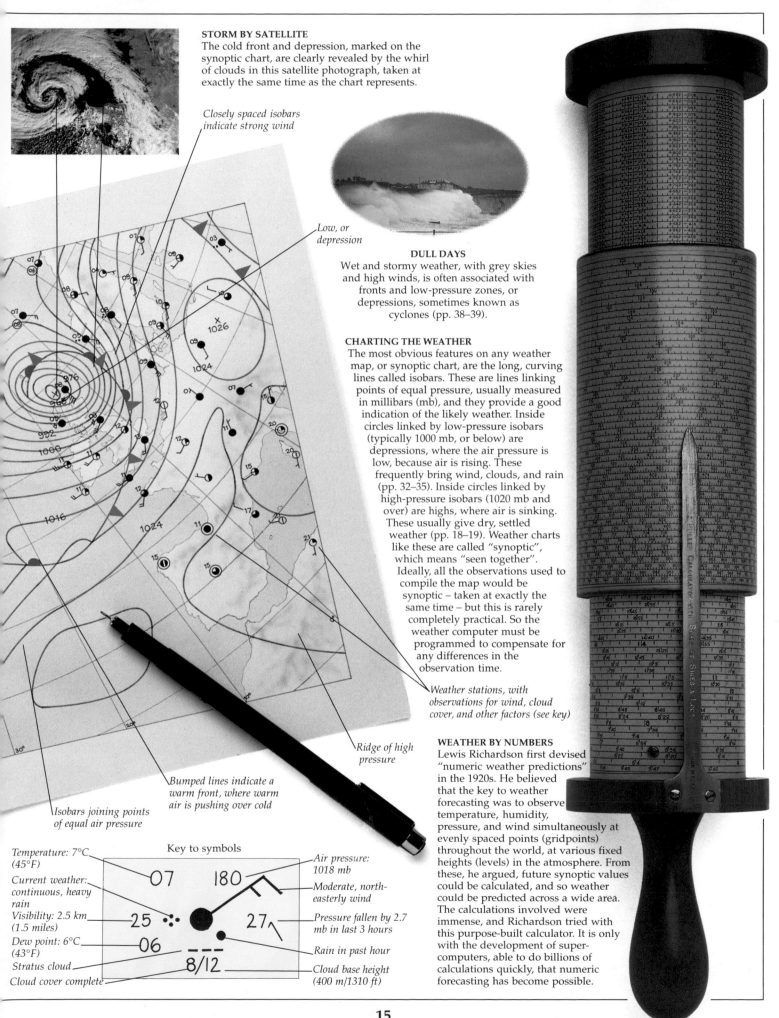

STORM BY SATELLITE
The cold front and depression, marked on the synoptic chart, are clearly revealed by the whirl of clouds in this satellite photograph, taken at exactly the same time as the chart represents.

Closely spaced isobars indicate strong wind

Low, or depression

DULL DAYS
Wet and stormy weather, with grey skies and high winds, is often associated with fronts and low-pressure zones, or depressions, sometimes known as cyclones (pp. 38–39).

CHARTING THE WEATHER
The most obvious features on any weather map, or synoptic chart, are the long, curving lines called isobars. These are lines linking points of equal pressure, usually measured in millibars (mb), and they provide a good indication of the likely weather. Inside circles linked by low-pressure isobars (typically 1000 mb, or below) are depressions, where the air pressure is low, because air is rising. These frequently bring wind, clouds, and rain (pp. 32–35). Inside circles linked by high-pressure isobars (1020 mb and over) are highs, where air is sinking. These usually give dry, settled weather (pp. 18–19). Weather charts like these are called "synoptic", which means "seen together". Ideally, all the observations used to compile the map would be synoptic – taken at exactly the same time – but this is rarely completely practical. So the weather computer must be programmed to compensate for any differences in the observation time.

Weather stations, with observations for wind, cloud cover, and other factors (see key)

Ridge of high pressure

Bumped lines indicate a warm front, where warm air is pushing over cold

Isobars joining points of equal air pressure

WEATHER BY NUMBERS
Lewis Richardson first devised "numeric weather predictions" in the 1920s. He believed that the key to weather forecasting was to observe temperature, humidity, pressure, and wind simultaneously at evenly spaced points (gridpoints) throughout the world, at various fixed heights (levels) in the atmosphere. From these, he argued, future synoptic values could be calculated, and so weather could be predicted across a wide area. The calculations involved were immense, and Richardson tried with this purpose-built calculator. It is only with the development of super-computers, able to do billions of calculations quickly, that numeric forecasting has become possible.

Key to symbols

Temperature: 7°C (45°F)

Current weather: continuous, heavy rain

Visibility: 2.5 km (1.5 miles)

Dew point: 6°C (43°F)

Stratus cloud

Cloud cover complete

07   180

25   27

06

8/12

Air pressure: 1018 mb

Moderate, north-easterly wind

Pressure fallen by 2.7 mb in last 3 hours

Rain in past hour

Cloud base height (400 m/1310 ft)

The power of the sun

A closeup view of the sun, showing a violent storm erupting at the surface

18th-century carved ivory pocket sundial

WITHOUT THE SUN, there would be no weather. Light from the sun is the energy which fuels the world's great weather machine. Sunshine, wind, rain, fog, snow, hail, thunder – every type of weather happens because the heat of the sun keeps the atmosphere constantly in motion. But the power of the sun's rays to heat the air varies – across the world, through the day, and through the year. All these variations depend on the sun's height in the sky. When the sun is high in the sky, its rays strike the ground directly, and its heat is at a maximum. When it is low in the sky, the sun's rays strike the ground at an angle, and its heat is spread out over a wider area. It is largely because of these variations that we get hot weather and cold weather, hot places and cold places.

Gnomon

18th-century brass garden sundial

DAILY RHYTHMS *left and above*
The shadow cast by the sundial's needle, or "gnomon", shifts as the sun moves through the sky from sunrise to sunset, indicating the time of day. So too does the sun's power to heat the air vary through the day – with profound effects upon the weather we experience.

HOT SPOTS
Deserts occur wherever the air is very dry, so few clouds can form. The hottest deserts, like the Sahara, are in the tropics, but there are cold deserts in central Asia, far from the ocean.

 Mountain
Taiga: cold plains
Polar

Temperate
Mediterranean
Savannah: warm plains
Subtropical
Tropical
Desert

POLAR COLD
Vast areas of the Arctic and Antarctic, where it is always cold, are covered in a permanent sheet of ice, up to 300 m (985 ft) thick.

THE WORLD'S CLIMATES
Because the Earth's surface is curved, the sun's rays strike different parts at different angles, dividing the world into distinct climate zones, each with its own typical weather. (A place's climate is just its average weather.) The world's hottest places are in the tropics, straddling the equator, for here the sun is almost overhead at noon. The coldest places are at the poles, where even at noon, the sun is so low in the sky that its power is spread out over a wide area. In between these extremes lie the temperate zones. Within these broad zones, however, climates vary considerably according to such factors as proximity to oceans and mountains, and height above sea level.

Earth *Moon*

SEASONED WEATHER

In the tropics, there are often just two seasons in the year, one wet and one dry. In hot deserts, there are no real seasons, for the weather changes little through the year. But in the temperate zones, the weather passes through four distinct phases during the year – spring, summer, autumn, winter. Shown here is the illustration for summer in the beautiful illuminated manuscripts drawn for the French Duc de Berry in the 14th century.

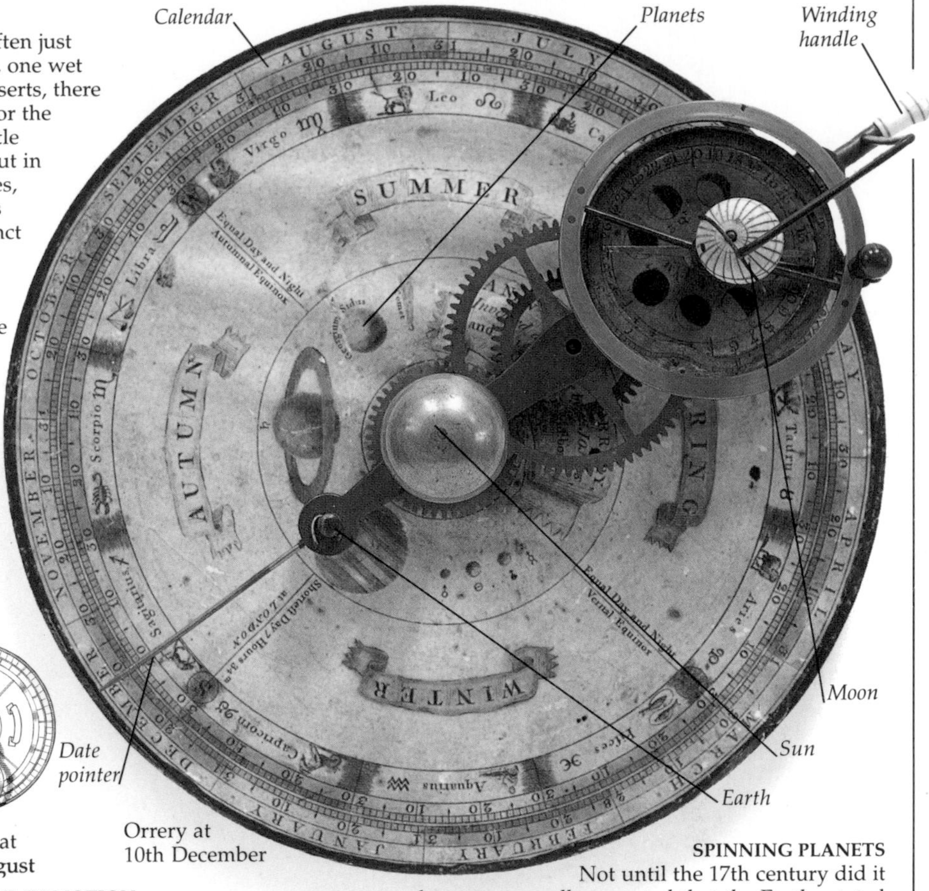

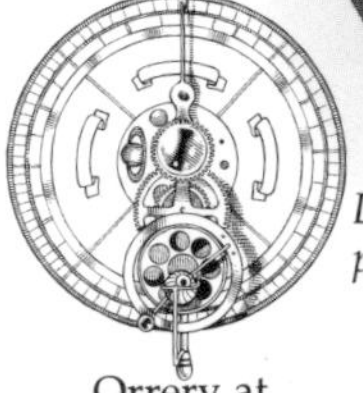

Calendar

Planets

Winding handle

Moon

Sun

Earth

Date pointer

Orrery at 5th August

Orrery at 10th December

WORLD IN MOTION

As the Earth journeys annually around the sun, our view of both the sun and distant stars changes constantly, as this old astronomical device, called an armillary sphere, was designed to show. The weather we experience depends to a large extent on our view of the sun.

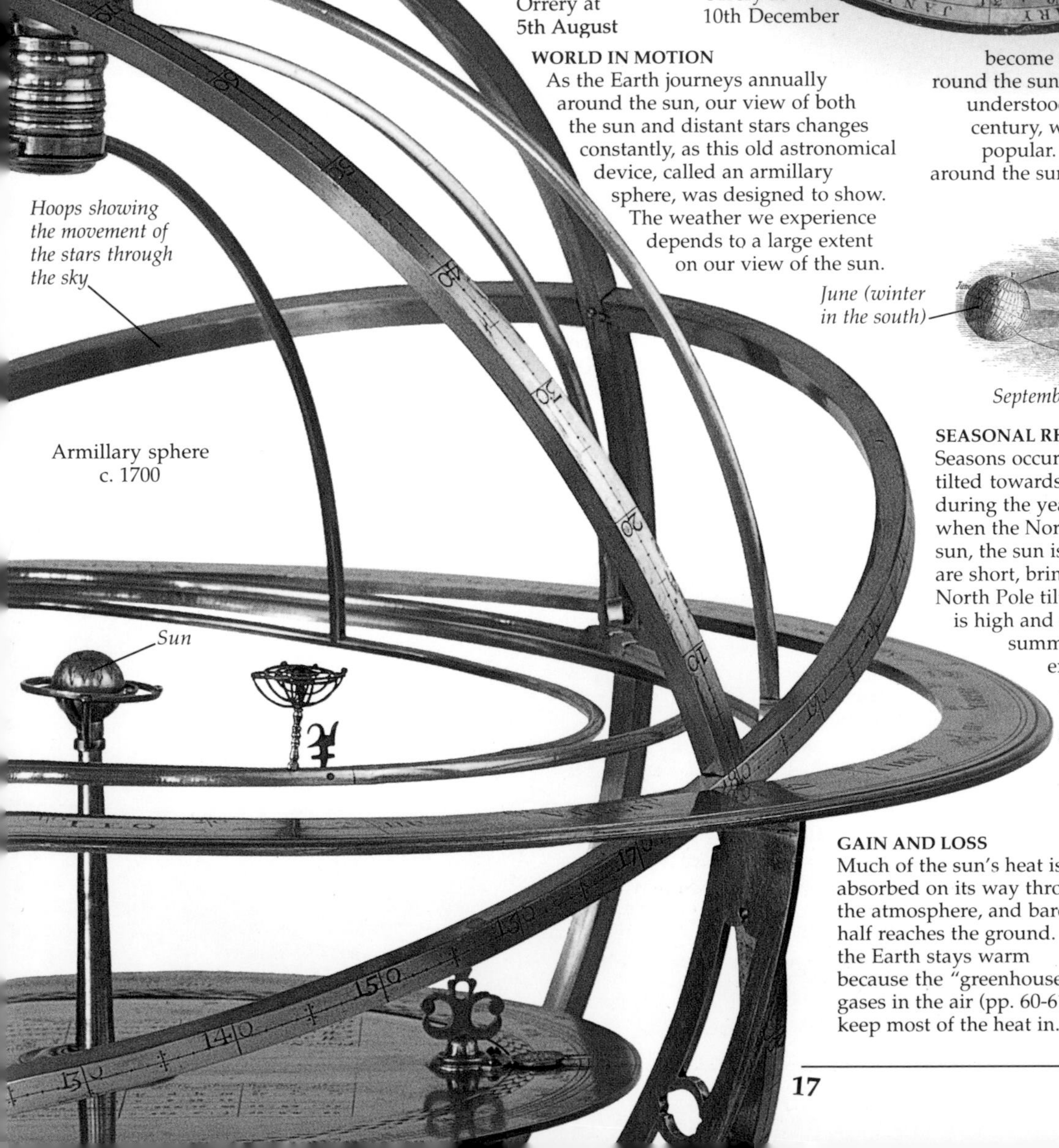

Hoops showing the movement of the stars through the sky

Armillary sphere c. 1700

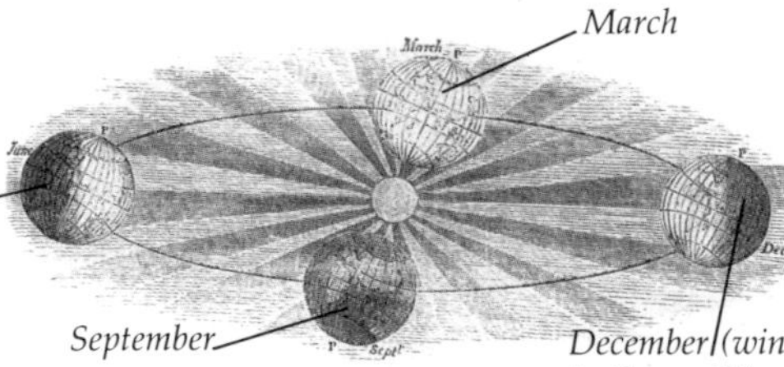

Sun

SPINNING PLANETS

Not until the 17th century did it become generally accepted that the Earth rotated round the sun, not the reverse. Only then was it finally understood why we have seasons. In the following century, wind-up models called orreries were very popular. These reproduce the Earth's true motion around the sun and its relationship to the four seasons.

March

June (winter in the south)

September

December (winter in the north)

SEASONAL RHYTHMS

Seasons occur because different parts of the Earth are tilted towards the sun as it moves around the sun during the year. In the northern hemisphere when the North Pole tilts away from the sun, the sun is low in the sky and days are short, bringing winter. When the North Pole tilts towards the sun, the sun is high and days are long, bringing summer. Between these two extremes lie spring and autumn. In the southern hemisphere, the seasons are precisely the opposite.

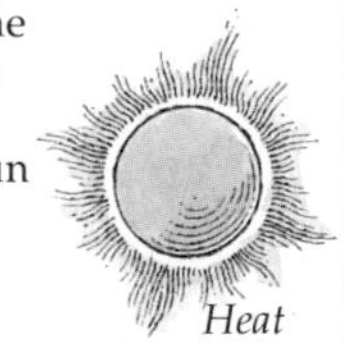

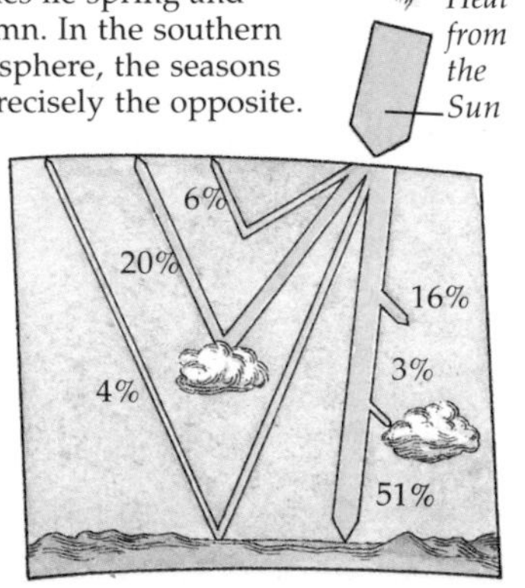

Heat from the Sun

GAIN AND LOSS

Much of the sun's heat is absorbed on its way through the atmosphere, and barely half reaches the ground. But the Earth stays warm because the "greenhouse" gases in the air (pp. 60-61) keep most of the heat in.

6%

20%

16%

4%

3%

51%

A sunny day

Over much of the world, sunny weather and almost cloudless skies are common, especially in summer. Indeed, in the eastern Sahara, the sun is covered by clouds for less than 100 hours of the year. Sunny weather is actually the most stable, persistent kind of weather, and a day that starts sunny and cloudless is likely to stay that way. Clouds form only when there is enough moisture in the air – and enough movement to carry the moisture high into the atmosphere. If the air is both dry and calm, clouds will not form, nor will they be blown in from elsewhere. This is why sunny weather is often associated with high atmospheric pressure (pp. 14–15), where the air is slowly sinking and virtually still. In summer, high pressure can persist for a long time – as the sinking air pushes out any new influences – and the weather remains warm and sunny for days on end.

The hottest place in the world is Dallol in Ethiopia, where annual temperatures average 34.4°C (94°F).

GROWING LIGHT
Green plants need plenty of sunshine, for all their energy for growth comes directly from the sun. Cells in their leaves contain chlorophyll which converts sunlight into chemical energy by photosynthesis.

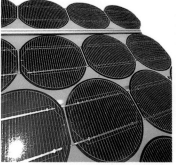

SUN GOD
So important was reliable sunshine in ancient times – not only for heat and light but for ripening crops – that many early civilizations worshipped the sun. The Aztecs of Mexico, in particular, built vast temples to the sun god Tonatuich, and made many bloody sacrifices, both animal and human, to persuade him to shine brightly on them.

BURNING RECORD
Meteorologists usually record hours of sunshine on a simple device called a Campbell-Stokes sunshine recorder. This has a glass ball to focus the sun's rays on to a strip of card so that they burn the card. As the sun moves round during the day, so do the scorch marks on the paper, giving a complete scorch mark record of the day's sunshine. This early recorder (viewed from above) was made by the Irish physicist Sir George Stokes in 1881.

Image of sun reflected in glass orb

SOLAR POWER
Nearly all our energy comes from the sun. Solar cells let us tap this energy directly, using light-sensitive crystals to convert sunshine into electricity. Solar power is only practical in places with plenty of sunshine.

Burn marks on card

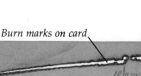

1024 mb   Full sun   Light
                       wind

Wisps of high cirrus cloud, made entirely of ice. These may be the remnants of a vanished storm cloud, since ice vapourizes more slowly than water. But they could signal the onset of a warm front (pp. 32-33)

Remnants of contrails

Contrails left in the wake of jet planes, especially in cold, dry air. Made of ice, like cirrus clouds, contrails form when the hot gases that shoot out behind the jet hit cool air and rise rapidly. As they rise, they expand and cool so sharply that water droplets soon condense and then freeze

Small, short-lived, fluffy cumulus clouds may be formed here and there by rising warm air currents

Low-level haze, especially over urban areas. Winds may be too light to disperse smoke and dust, and, if the pressure is high, a temperature inversion may trap water vapour and pollutants in a layer just above the ground (pp. 48-49)

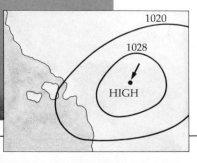

1020
1028
HIGH

Frost and ice

KEEPING THE COLD OUT
In some parts of the world, frosty nights are characterized by the malevolent, spiky "Jack Frost", who leaves his icy finger marks on every window pane.

1020 mb

Full sun

Little wind

W<small>HEN A CALM, CLEAR, DRY NIGHT</small> follows a cold winter's day, a sharp frost may well descend on many places by morning. Temperatures rarely climb high in winter, when the sun is low in the sky during the day, and the nights are long. If the night sky is clear, too, then any heat retained in the ground can flow away quickly, allowing temperatures to plummet. Frosts are rare but by no means unheard of in the tropics – and almost continuous towards the poles. In Vostok, in Antarctica, temperatures average a bitter -57.8°C (-72°F). In the mid-latitudes, frosts occur whenever the conditions are right, more often inland than near the coast, where the sea tends to retain heat longer.

The low temperatures near the ground that bring a frost can also create fog (pp. 48–49). The moisture condenses in the cold air and hangs there, because there is little wind to disperse it. If the fog coats things with ice, it is called freezing fog

Thick coating of rime, a white ice formed when an icy wind blows over leaves, branches, and other surfaces. Temperatures usually have to be lower for rime than for hoar frost

ICING UP
High in the atmosphere, air temperatures are always below freezing, and the wings of high-flying aeroplanes can easily become coated with rime ice. This drastically affects their performance. Most jet airliners now have de-icing equipment.

COLD FRAME
Frost can create beautiful patterns of ice crystals. If the weather is especially severe, delicate traceries of "fern frost" may appear on the inside of windows. First, dew forms on the cold glass. Then, as some dewdrops cool below freezing point, they turn into ice crystals, encouraging more ice crystals to form.

HOAR THORNS
When water vapour touches a very cold surface, it can freeze instantly, leaving spiky needles of "hoar frost" on leaves and branches – and also on cars, for their metal bodies get very cold. Hoar frost tends to occur when the air temperature is around 0°C (32°F), and the ground is much colder – but the air must be moist to create the ice crystals.

Hoar frost coats freezing cold surfaces such as soil and metal with ice crystals

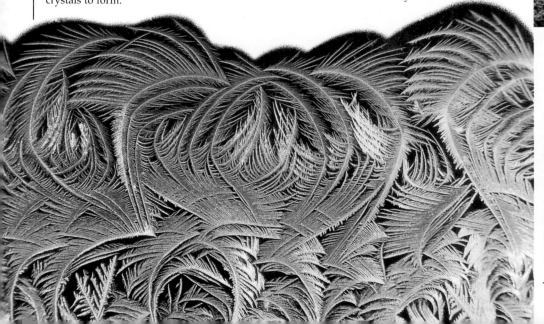

FROZEN ARCH
Arctic and Antarctic temperatures are perpetually below freezing, and ice can last hundreds of years. Sometimes vast chunks of ice, or icebergs, break off polar glaciers and float out to sea. They float because water becomes less dense when it freezes, but most of their bulk lies below the water.

Even though there is a mist near the ground, the sky above is clear, allowing heat to escape during the night

Frost is white because the crystals contain air

HIGH

LOW

ICY COATING (above)
When the conditions are cold enough, moisture from the air freezes, leaving the ground, leaves, branches, and many other surfaces coated with a thin layer of ice crystals, although sometimes frost can occur because heat is radiated from the ground on clear nights. Spring and autumn frosts often happen this way. In mid-winter, though, a chill polar wind may be enough to bring frost.

ICE HOUSE
Very low temperatures can produce spectacular ice effects. Most icicles form when cold nights freeze drips of melting snow. This house in Chicago, USA, got its remarkable coat of ice when firemen turned their hoses on it to put out a fire – on the coldest night in the city's history, when temperatures plummeted to -32°C (-26°F) on 10th January 1982.

MARKET ON ICE
In the early 1800s, the weather tended to be much colder than today. Frosts could be so hard that even the River Thames in London froze solid. The last "frost fair" held on the ice was in 1814, before the weather began to warm up.

Water in the air

EVEN ON THE SUNNIEST DAY, the horizon often shimmers indistinctly in a haze, and distant hills look soft and grey. Some haze is dust and pollution, but most is simply moisture in the air. Even over the hottest deserts, the atmosphere contains some moisture. Like a dry sponge, the air continually soaks up water that evaporates from oceans, lakes, and rivers, and transpires from trees, grass, and other plants. Most of the moisture is water vapour, a gas mixed invisibly into the air. When it cools enough, the moisture condenses into tiny droplets of water, forming the clouds, mist, and haze that continually girdle the Earth. Water vapour will form water droplets only if the air contains plenty of dust, smoke, and salt particles, called condensation nuclei, for it to condense on to. If the air is very pure, there will not be enough nuclei, so clouds and mist will not form.

DEW DROPS
Moisture condenses as air cools because the cooler the air is, the less water vapour it can hold. So as it cools down, air becomes nearer saturation – that is, the limit it can hold. Once it reaches this limit, called the dew point, water vapour condenses into droplets. After a cold night, dew drops can be seen sparkling on grass and spiders' webs.

Scale shows humidity

Human hair stretches in moist air and contracts in dry air

Hair hygrometer

WET HAIR
The moisture content of the air, called humidity, can be measured using a hair hygrometer. Meteorologists need to know how much water there is in the air, in proportion to the most water it can hold at that temperature and pressure. This is called relative humidity.

When the water level in the spout is high, pressure is low, and storms can be expected

Closed glass bulb

When working, the level of water in the weather glass would have been much higher

STORM GLASS
Like mercury in a barometer, water levels can be used to monitor air pressure. Though not accurate, "weather glasses" like this were cheaper to make than proper mercury barometers, and were quite common on small boats.

Gruß aus Villach

WEATHER HOUSE
Before weather forecasting was common, weather houses like this used to be popular. Actually, they are hair hygrometers. When the air is moist, a hair inside the house stretches and lets the man come out of the door. If the air is dry, the hair shrinks, pulling the man in and letting the woman pop out.

Wet bulb

Glass tube

Damp muslin cover

Scale

Dry bulb

WET AND DRY

Another method of measuring humidity is with a psychrometer, or wet and dry bulb thermometer. This instrument, shown left, is an antique version and not like those used today. The dry bulb measures air temperature normally. The wet bulb is surrounded by wet muslin. As water in the muslin evaporates, it takes heat from the bulb. The drier the air, the more water evaporates, and the cooler the wet bulb becomes. So the greater the difference in readings between the wet and dry bulbs, the lower the humidity.

SMALL MEASURES

This tiny pocket hygrometer – less than 4 cm (1 $^3/_5$ in) in diameter – uses human hair to work the needle and is surprisingly accurate. Instruments like this used to be very popular with walkers, who wanted to predict a shower.

MISTY MOUNTAINS

At night, the ground cools down gradually, and so cools the air above it. If the air temperature drops below its dew point, it becomes saturated, and water droplets condense into the air to form a mist. In mountain areas (pp. 52–53), mist will often gather in the valleys in the morning because cold air flows downhill in the night, and settles there.

WATER VISION

If it were not for the moisture in the air, we could nearly always see into the distance much more clearly. Fog and mist cut down visibility dramatically, but even on apparently clear days, there is often a slight haze in the air, making distant hills look pale and indistinct.

DAMP TRADE

Many activities, such as silk-making in China, depend upon the humidity of the air. If the air is not damp enough, the caterpillars will not spin the thread properly.

GROWING RAINDROPS

When rain falls on a window, only the biggest drops run down the pane. Unless a raindrop is big to start with, a phenomenon known as surface tension will hold it on the glass until another drop falls in the same place. Then the tension will be broken, and the drops will run down the pane in rivulets. In the same way, tiny droplets of water in a cloud will only start to fall as rain once they are large and heavy enough to over-come air resistance.

Rain drop just large enough to overcome tension

Small raindrops held on glass by surface tension

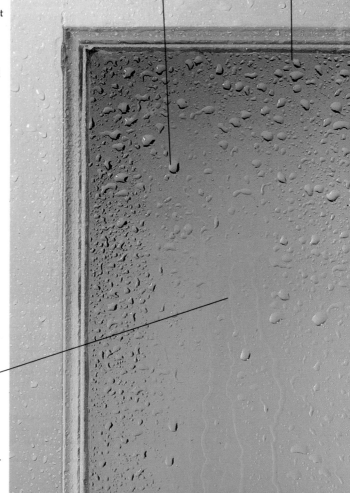

Rivulet gathering in other drops on its path

A cloudy day

CLOUDY SKIES ARE RARE OVER DRY DESERTS. But in more humid areas, the weather may stay dull and overcast for days on end. Sometimes, fluffy, short-lived cumulus clouds (pp. 28–29) heap up enough to form a dense bank, shutting out the sun. More often, though, persistently cloudy skies are associated with layered, or "stratus", clouds. Clouds like these build up gradually over a wide area when a warm, moist wind meets colder air. As this warm air rides slowly up over cold air, moisture steadily condenses from the air as it cools – creating a vast blanket of cloud that can be several hundred metres thick and stretch for hundreds of kilometres.

MEASURING CLOUD HEIGHT
The Victorians calculated the height of clouds by using cameras and giant tripods, but meteorologists nowadays use laser beams pointed at the base of the cloud to judge its height. Cloud cover, however, is worked out visually, by estimating roughly what proportion of the sky is obscured by the cloud directly overhead – usually in tenths or eighths.

THREE KINDS OF CLOUD
On some cloudy days, nothing but a thin blanket of low stratus is visible. On other days, many kinds of clouds may be seen at different heights in the sky. Thin sheets of stratus may not be enough to stop warm updraughts of air, or thermals, developing and cumulus clouds growing (pp. 24–25), especially if the sun is strong. In this picture, taken near mountains close to a weak cold front (pp. 34–35), there are not only stratus and cumulus, but also a third type, called lenticular clouds, formed by waves in the wind in the lee of mountains (pp. 54–55).

Small cumulus clouds are unlikely to give much rain – although there might be light showers later in the day

Stratus cloud

Thermals (pp. 24–25) rising beneath cumulus clouds

UPS AND DOWNS
Cumulus clouds indicate to glider pilots the presence of updraughts, or thermals, that they need for climbing. These are common over ploughed fields and other warm areas of soil, but over comparatively cold bodies of water, such as lakes, the thermals will not form, and gliders sink back down towards the ground. The same thing happens if thick layers of medium-height or high cloud cover the sky and cut off the warmth of the sunlight from the ground.

MARES' TAILS
Cirrus clouds form high in the sky where the atmosphere [is] so cold that they are made entirely from ice crystals. Stro[ng] winds blow the crystals into wispy "mares' tails".

Cirrostr[atus]
into [a]
appear[s]
or n[...]

Mainly ice crystals

HIGH, FLUFFY CLO[UDS]
Cirrocumulus are [...] cloud. They consis[t...] clouds, and often [...] and ripples, know[n...] they look like the [...]

Cloud moves from left to right

Strong updraughts carry billows of cloud high into the atmosphere

Mixture of ice crystals and water

SHOWER CLOUDS *left*
Bigger and darker than cumulus, cumulonimbus usually bring showers of rain – nimbus means "rain" in Latin. Sometimes they grow huge and unleash sudden, gigantic thunderstorms.

Violent up[draughts and] downdraug[hts...] wall of clou[d...] hailstones [...]

Mainly wat[er]

Air dra[...]

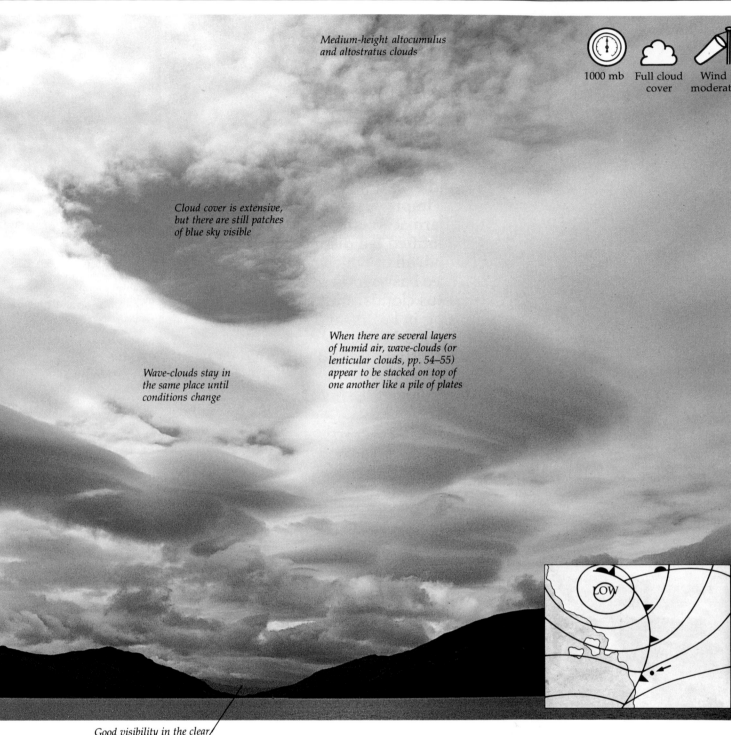

Medium-height altocumulus and altostratus clouds

Cloud cover is extensive, but there are still patches of blue sky visible

When there are several layers of humid air, wave-clouds (or lenticular clouds, pp. 54–55) appear to be stacked on top of one another like a pile of plates

Wave-clouds stay in the same place until conditions change

Good visibility in the clear air beneath the clouds

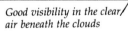

SMOOTH OR LUMPY
In *The Beauty of the Heavens* (London, 1845), the Victorian painter Charles F. Blunt depicted two main groups of clouds: cumulus (detail, left), which are heaped clouds formed by the rise of individual bubbles of air (pp. 24–25); and cirrostratus (detail, right), where whole layers of air are forced to rise, for example at a front (pp. 32–33), forming widespread sheets of cloud.

Clouds c

LUKE HOWARD (1772–1864)
A keen amateur meteorologist, Howard devised his system by regularly observing clouds and analyzing their shapes and heights.

CLOUDS FLOAT A
shapes, sizes, and
mares' tails to tow
thunderclouds. T
variety of clouds
classification coul
has been found to
by the English ph
1803. Howard ide
of clou
on thr
cumul
formir
cirrus
prove
that it
meteo

Tempe

TRANSLUCENT CLOUD
Altostratus are high, thin sheets of cloud that can often completely cover the sky, so that the sun looks as if it is seen through misty glass. At a warm front (pp. 32–33), lower, thicker, nimbostratus, rain clouds normally follow.

Cloud	Height
Cirrus	12 km
Cirrostratus	11 km
Cirrocumulus	10 km
Altostratus	9 km
Altocumulus	8 km
	7 km
Stratocumulus	6 km
Cumulus	5 km
	4 km
Cumulonimbus	3 km
	2 km
Stratus	1 km
Nimbostratus	Sea level

Temperature here 0°C (

CLOUD HEIGHTS
Cirrus-type clouds, including cirrocumulus and cirrostratus, form at the top of the troposphere, where it is coldest. Altostratus and altocumulus are found at medium heights, stratocumulus, stratus, nimbostratus, and cumulus closer to the ground (pp. 6–7). Cumulonimbus may reach up through the whole troposphere.

Monsoon

TROPICAL STORM
The monsoon can lash tropical coasts with intense rain, wind, thunder, and lightning.

FOR SIX MONTHS of the year, most of India is parched and dry. But, every May, the monsoon comes. A moist wind starts to blow in from the Indian Ocean and the skies over the southwest coast grow dark with clouds. For six months, showers of torrential rain sweep north over the country, right up to the foothills of the Himalayas – until, in October, the southwest wind dies down and the rains slacken. By the end of the year, the land is dry once more. The monsoon is especially marked in India, but similar rainy seasons occur in many other places in the tropics, including northeast Australia, East Africa, and the southern United States.

DRAGON'S BREATH
The monsoon rains are vital for agriculture in most of Asia. To the Chinese their importance was symbolized by the dragon, a creature of the heavens and of the rivers – at times violent, but also the bringer of the precious gift of water.

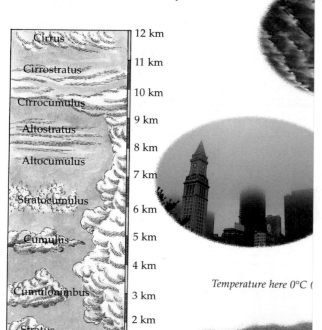

AFTER THE DELUGE
Monsoon rain can be so intense that floods are frequent. In India and Bangladesh, the delta of the river Ganges is in particular danger of being flooded, especially if a storm surge occurs at the same time (pp. 44–45).

The monsoon brings some of the world's most torrential rains

Band of rain moving rapidly across open grassland

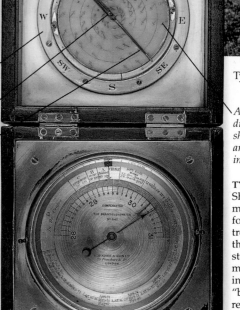

Wind disc for tracking the path of the typhoon

Heavy needle lines up with the normal path of storms in the region

Thin needle indicates safe course away from the storm

Typhoon barometer

Arrows on the disc for the direction of the wind over the ship. The disc is turned until an arrow crosses the heavy needle in the right direction

TYPHOON TRACKER
Ships at sea around many monsoon regions often fall foul of ferocious, fast-moving tropical cyclones. To help them track the path of the storm and steer a safe course, many ships used to carry an instrument like this, called a "baryocyclometer". Now most rely on broadcast warnings.

High cumulonimbus clouds

Large cumulonimbus clouds pile up against high ground as the monsoon blows inland

Mountains force the monsoon upward causing even more rain: Cherrapunji in the Assam mountains is one of the wettest places in the world

Some areas may stay dry and parched even while neighbouring areas are being drenched

THE MONSOON COMES

Monsoons are like giant sea breezes (pp. 56–57). The rains begin when summer sun heats up tropical continents far faster than the oceans around. Warm air rising over land draws in cool, moist air from the sea, and rain-bearing winds gradually push farther inland. A monsoon's onset is hard to predict, and sometimes it fails to bring any rain to the hot, drought-stricken lands that year. Then crops fail, with a great danger of famine. Asian monsoons may be triggered off when westerly jet streams in the upper air swing north over the Himalayas.

MONSOON REGION

Monsoons affect large areas of the tropics and the sub-tropics from northeast Australia to the Caribbean. Asian monsoons are the most marked, because Asia is so vast.

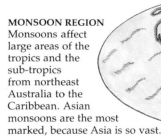

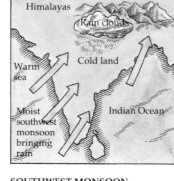

SOUTHWEST MONSOON

The hot, dry lands of Asia draw warm air, laden with moisture, in from the Indian Ocean during the early summer.

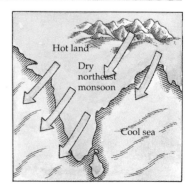

NORTHEAST MONSOON

The cold, dry winter air spreads out from central Asia, bringing chilly, dusty conditions to the lands around.

A snowy day

IN THE DEPTHS OF WINTER, driving snow and blizzards may fall from the same grey clouds and fronts that in summer brought welcome showers. Outside the tropics, most rain starts off as snow, melting as it drops into warmer air. When snow falls, the air is just cold enough to let the flakes flutter to the ground before they melt. Sometimes, snow can be falling on the mountaintop while down in the valley it is raining. People often say the weather is "too cold for snow", and there is some truth in this, since very cold air may not hold enough moisture for any kind of precipitation (pp. 22-23). In fact, more snow falls in a year in southern Canada and the northern USA than at the North Pole. The heaviest snowfalls occur when the air temperature is hovering around freezing – which is why snow can be hard to forecast, because a rise in temperature of just a few degrees above freezing may bring rain instead.

ST. BERNARDS TO THE RESCUE
Freshly fallen snow contains so much air that people can survive for a long time beneath it.

Under very cold conditions snow remains loose and powdery, and is often whipped up by the wind

Fresh snow can contain as much as 90-95 per cent air, and acts as an insulator, protecting the ground from much colder temperatures above the surface

RIVERS OF ICE AND AIR
Snow accumulates on high ground where temperatures are low. It becomes compacted into ice, which slowly flows down valleys as glaciers. The air above large ice-caps becomes very cold and heavy, and follows the same paths, bringing icy winds to the lowlands beneath.

A COLD BLANKET
Once snow has covered the ground, it is often slow to melt, because it reflects away most of the sunlight. If the surface melts partially and then refreezes, the snow-cover will last even longer. Only the arrival of a warm air-mass is really effective in melting the snow.

SNOWFLAKES
Snowflakes occur in an infinite variety of shapes, and no-one has ever found two the same. All natural snowflakes are six-sided, and consist of ice crystals which are flat plates, although rarer forms like needles and columns are sometimes found.

THE SNOWFLAKE MAN
W. A. Bentley was an American farmer who spent every possible moment out in the cold, photographing snowflakes through a microscope. Over 40 years he obtained many thousands of photographs.

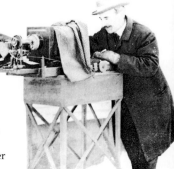

"Tablecloth" of stratus cloud caused by gentle airflow over the mountains

On average, 30.5 cm (12 in) of snow is equal to 2.54 cm (1 in) of rain

Harder surface crust caused by melting and refreezing

Eddies in the wind always cause more snow to fall in one place than in another, leading to drifts, which tend to grow larger and larger

LOW

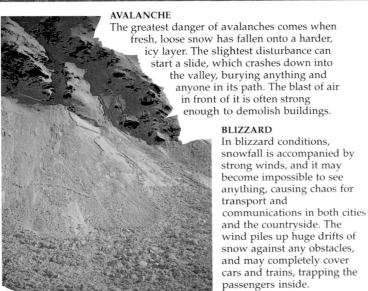

AVALANCHE

The greatest danger of avalanches comes when fresh, loose snow has fallen onto a harder, icy layer. The slightest disturbance can start a slide, which crashes down into the valley, burying anything and anyone in its path. The blast of air in front of it is often strong enough to demolish buildings.

BLIZZARD

In blizzard conditions, snowfall is accompanied by strong winds, and it may become impossible to see anything, causing chaos for transport and communications in both cities and the countryside. The wind piles up huge drifts of snow against any obstacles, and may completely cover cars and trains, trapping the passengers inside.

Whirling winds

Tornadoes go by many names – twisters, whirlwinds, and more. Wherever they strike, these whirling spirals of wind leave a trail of unbelievable destruction. They roar past in just a few minutes, tossing people, cars, and strong buildings high into the air, then smashing them to the ground. Meteorological instruments rarely survive to tell what conditions are really like in a tornado. Winds probably race around the outside at over 400 kph (240 mph), while pressure at the centre plunges several hundred millibars lower than outside. This creates a kind of funnel, or vortex, that acts like a giant vacuum cleaner sucking things into the air, tearing the tops off trees, and blowing out windows. Tornadoes hang down like an elephant's trunk from giant thunderclouds, and may strike wherever thunderstorms occur.

MILD SPIN
Tornadoes are especially violent in the central USA, but they can occur anywhere there are thunderstorms, as this engraving of an English whirlwind shows.

Supercell cloud

Cloud base

1 SWIRLING COLUMN
Tornadoes start deep within vast thunderclouds, where a column of strongly rising warm air is set spinning by high winds streaming through the cloud's top. As air is sucked into this swirling column, or mesocyclone, it spins very fast, stretching thousands of metres up and down through the cloud, with a corkscrewing funnel descending from the cloud's base – the tornado.

CROP CIRCLES
For centuries, it has been a mystery why perfect circles of flattened crops appear at random in the summer. A few people believe that it may be whirling winds which cause them.

2 WHIRLING DERVISH
Soon the funnel touches down, and the tremendous updraught in its centre swirls dust, debris, cars, and people high into the sky. Chunks of wood and other objects become deadly missiles as they are hurled through the air by the ferocious winds. A tornado deals destruction very selectively – reducing houses in its path to matchwood and rubble, yet leaving those just a few metres outside its path completely untouched. Sometimes a tornado will whirl things high into the air, then set them gently down, unharmed, hundreds of metres away.

46

WATERSPOUT

When a tornado occurs over the sea, it becomes a waterspout. These often last longer than tornadoes, but tend to be gentler, with wind speeds less than 80 kph (50 mph). This may be because water is heavier than air, and the strong temperature contrasts needed to create violent updraughts are less marked over water than land.

DUSTY MENACE

Unlike tornadoes and waterspouts which spin down from clouds, "dust devils" are formed in the desert by columns of hot air whirling up from the ground. Far weaker than tornadoes, they can still cause damage. Whirling devils also occur over snow and water, although these can start as violent eddies whipping up from the surface.

FLYING ROOFS *left and above*

In the strong winds of tornadoes, the roofs of houses generate lift, just like the wings of a plane. When the roof is whisked away, the rest of the house disintegrates. Stronger roofs, more firmly anchored to the buildings beneath, would prevent a great deal of damage.

Funnel touching down in a whirling spray of dust and debris

3 SPINNING VORTEX

For a moment, the funnel has lifted away from the ground, and the houses beneath are safe. But at any instant it may touch down again. This is a large tornado, and within it there is not just one spinning vortex but several, each revolving around the rim of the main one.

A day of weather

THE WEATHER CAN CHANGE dramatically during the course of a single day. Sometimes these daily changes can be more striking than any long-term variations. In many tropical regions, the same marked changes in the weather occur regularly day after day, where fine, sunny mornings are almost always followed by a massive build-up of thunderclouds as the sun stirs up strong updraughts. Usually this is followed by a brief deluge in the afternoon and a clear dusk. A similar sequence often occurs in mid-latitudes if the weather is warm and stable. In these areas regular daily changes are often overpowered by the passage of a depression, which can swing the weather from warm sunshine to icy rain in a few hours.

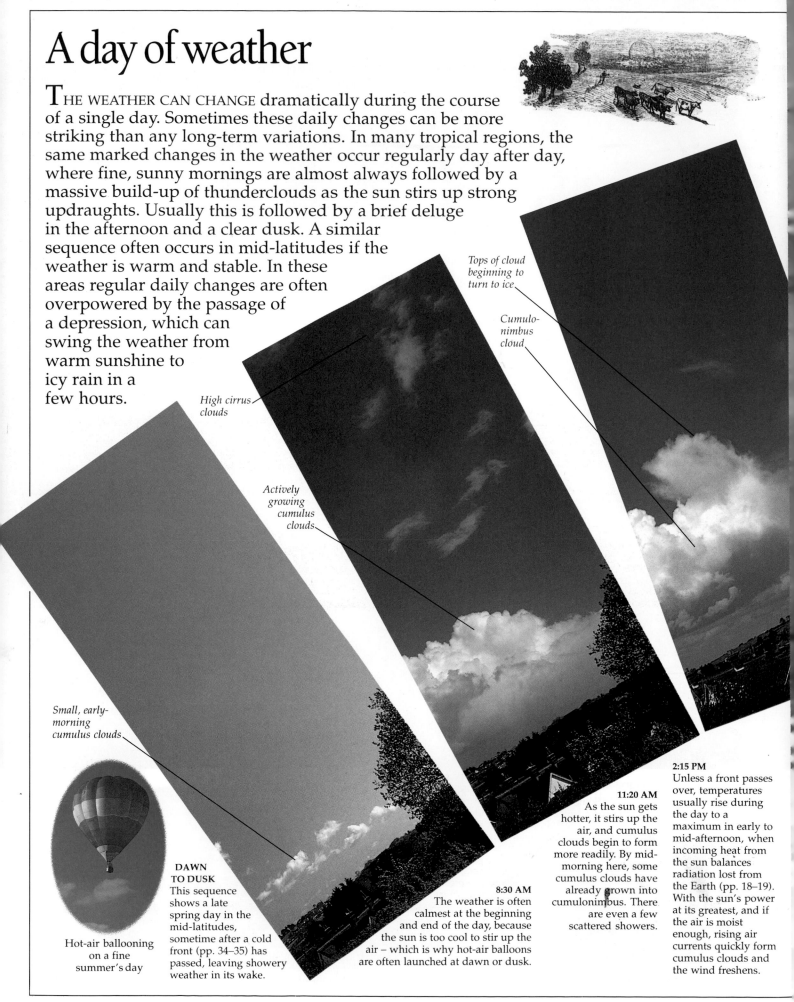

Tops of cloud beginning to turn to ice

Cumulo-nimbus cloud

High cirrus clouds

Actively growing cumulus clouds

Small, early-morning cumulus clouds

Hot-air ballooning on a fine summer's day

DAWN TO DUSK
This sequence shows a late spring day in the mid-latitudes, sometime after a cold front (pp. 34–35) has passed, leaving showery weather in its wake.

8:30 AM
The weather is often calmest at the beginning and end of the day, because the sun is too cool to stir up the air – which is why hot-air balloons are often launched at dawn or dusk.

11:20 AM
As the sun gets hotter, it stirs up the air, and cumulus clouds begin to form more readily. By mid-morning here, some cumulus clouds have already grown into cumulonimbus. There are even a few scattered showers.

2:15 PM
Unless a front passes over, temperatures usually rise during the day to a maximum in early to mid-afternoon, when incoming heat from the sun balances radiation lost from the Earth (pp. 18–19). With the sun's power at its greatest, and if the air is moist enough, rising air currents quickly form cumulus clouds and the wind freshens.

Icy head of cloud spread out by high level winds

Sky thick with cloud

Sky starting to lighten behind cloud

Rain heavy in places

Rain

3:00 PM
By mid-afternoon, clouds can build up to such an extent that thunderstorms occur. Here, clusters of clouds have joined together to make even larger storms, with thunder and lightning, very heavy rain, and hail nearby, even if not overhead.

3:45 PM
The sky is still darkened by a gigantic, grey cumulonimbus cloud, its top hidden by the widespread lower clouds around the edge of the storm, which is now upon us. Gusts of wind give warning of the downdraughts and torrential rain to come.

5:15 PM
The heavy clouds are beginning to lift and move away, although rain is still falling. Sunlight strikes through beneath the edge of the cloud, illuminating the raindrops and creating a rainbow. The worst of the storm is over.

Extra, pinkish-violet bows inside the primary bow

CASTLES IN THE AIR
In the right conditions, a layer of warm air may form over a cold sea. On the Italian island of Sicily, this can produce a mirage about mid-morning called "Fata Morgana". Distorted images of distant objects appear, looking like castles or tall buildings. They are created when the warm air bends light rays from images of objects normally invisible beyond the horizon.

7:00 PM
By sunset, the wind has dropped and the band of thunderstorms and showers has moved away, leaving only a few scattered cumulus. In contrast to the clear sky of the morning, increasing middle-level clouds show that a weak trough of low pressure is approaching from the west.

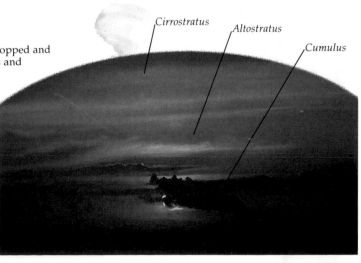

Cirrostratus

Altostratus

Cumulus

Weather on the plains

THE GREAT PLAINS of North America, the Steppes of Russia, the Pampas of South America, the grasslands of Australia – these and other vast, flat plains of the world experience weather that is very different from that in the mountains (pp. 52–53). Far from the sea, or cut off from it by high mountains, plains tend to have hot summers and cold winters, and receive little rain. Fronts (pp. 32–35) are broken up by mountain ranges, or lose their energy long before they reach the heart of the plains. What rain there is falls mostly in the summer when strong sun stirs up heavy showers and thunderstorms. In winter, rainfall is rare, although autumn snowstorms may deposit a covering that lasts until spring. In the shadow of mountain ranges, many plains are so dry that only scrub, or grass, can grow.

WINTER HUNTERS
Millions of buffalo once roamed the vast grasslands of North America and provided rich hunting for the many plains Indian tribes, who were well adapted to the cold winters. They would wear snowshoes when hunting to stop their feet sinking into the snow.

HOT BLAST
Where plains are in the lee of mountains they are often subject to hot winds, warmed as they descend from mountains. The Chinook of the North American Rockies, and the parching Arabian Simoom, shown in this engraving, are typical.

WAVE–CLOUDS
High mountain ranges often disturb winds blowing across them, and set up a pattern of waves that do not move, but hang in the same place in the upper atmosphere. Bands of stationary cloud may form in the crest of each wave.

Skies are often clear, giving hot summers and cold winters

EXTREME WEATHER
Far from any source of moisture, skies over the plains are often brilliantly clear and blue. This causes natural extremes in temperature between summer and winter, day and night. Winters on the plains are bitter, with temperatures well below freezing and severe frosts for many weeks. In summer, temperatures drop once the sun goes down.

PARCHED LANDS
Most of the world's great deserts are plains, such as North America's Nevada. Air subsiding over the desert warms as it descends, creating parched conditions, and then moves outwards, preventing moist air from entering. Mountain ranges produce dry "rainshadows" on their lee (downwind) side.

1000 mb   Some cloud cover   Strong wind

Smooth, lens-shaped "lenticular" wave-clouds often form in bands in the lee of mountain ranges, sometimes building up like piles of plates

With little to slow them down, the dry winds can be very strong in the plains

Low rainfall leads to scrubby, stunted vegetation

LOW

HIGH

SIZZLING SUMMERS

Summer on the plains can be extremely hot. In Death Valley, California (above), temperatures reached 56.7°C (134°F) in 1913. In Queensland, Australia, temperatures soared nearly as high at 53.1°C (127.6°F) in 1889. The highest temperature ever recorded is 58°C (136.4°F) in Libya in 1922.

DUST TO DUST

Far from the sea, plains lands are sensitive to climate changes. Strengthening westerly winds in the early 20th century increased the Rocky Mountains' rainshadow effect on the prairies. Drought in the 1930s brought disaster to vast areas, creating a "Dust Bowl" and forcing many families to leave their farms.

Weather by the sea

THE PRESENCE OF SO MUCH WATER GIVES weather by the sea its own particular characteristics. Winds blowing in off the sea are naturally moister than those blowing off the land. So coastal areas tend to be noticeably wetter than inland areas – especially if they face into the prevailing wind (pp. 42–43). They can be cloudier, too. Cumulus clouds (pp. 24–25), for instance, usually form inland only during the day, but on coasts facing the wind, they drift overhead at night as well, when cold winds blow in over the warm sea. Sometimes, these clouds bring localized showers to coastal areas. Fogs too can form at sea in the same way, and creep a little way inland. At daybreak the sea is often shrouded in a thick mist which only disperses as the wind changes, or the sun's heat begins to dry it up. The overall effect of all this water is to make weather in coastal areas generally less extreme than farther inland. Because the sea retains heat well, nights tend to be warmer on the coast, with winters milder, and summers slightly cooler. Frosts are rare on sea coasts in the mid-latitudes.

Frequent, salt-laden winds blowing from the sea dry the exposed sides of trees and shrubs, killing leaves and buds so the plants look as though they are leaning into the wind

LOW

OUT FOR A BLOW
Seaside resorts can often be quite windy, as this postcard from the early 20th century acknowledges. Not only does the open sea provide no obstacle to winds blowing off the sea, but temperature differences between land and sea can generate stiff breezes.

CLEAR COAST
This picture shows the coast of Oregon in the northwest USA, but it is typical of west coasts everywhere in the mid-latitudes. Deep depressions are common at this latitude and here a cold front (pp. 34–35) has just passed over, moving inland. An overhang of cloud lingers in the upper air from the front itself, and cumulus clouds are still growing in its wake. Further showers are clearly on their way. As the front moves inland, it may well produce progressively less rain, because there is less moisture available to feed its progress.

COASTAL FOG
Sea fog is an advection fog (pp. 48–49), which tends to persist until the direction of the wind changes, because the sea is slow to heat up. Off the coast of Newfoundland in Canada (left), where warm westerly winds blow over a sea cooled by currents flowing down from the Arctic, thick fogs can linger for days on end.

1000 mb | A little cloud cover | Strong wind

WIND AND WAVES
The winds that help windsurfers skim across the surface of the sea may often be locally generated sea breezes. But the waves they ride may be created by winds thousands of kilometres away. Waves are whipped up by the wind when air turbulence over the water creates little pockets of low and high pressure that suck and push on the water. Just how big the waves are depends on the strength of the wind, how long it blows, and the "fetch" – that is, how far it blows over the water.

Lingering clouds from cold front

Growing cumulus clouds

Visibility tends to be good on coasts, partly because winds are stronger, but mainly because over the sea the air is much cleaner and there are far fewer small smoke and dust particles on which water can condense

Lack of "white horses" on the waves shows the wind is only light

Waves begin to break in shallow water – where the water is less than twice as deep as the wave

Warmer air from over the sea is drawn over the land to replace the cool air that is sinking

Land cools quickly

Sea cools slowly

Sinking air over the land drives air seawards on the surface, creating a land breeze

Nighttime land breeze

Air pushed out to sea at high altitude increases the air pressure over the cool sea

Air rising over the warm sea pushes air at high altitude towards the land

Air sinks over the cool sea

Sinking air over the sea and rising air over the land drive sea air shore-wards, creating a stiff sea breeze at the surface

Air rises over the warm land about 1 km (1/2 mile) above the ground

Land warms up quickly in the sun

Sea warms up only slowly

Daytime sea breeze

Land and sea breezes

A marked characteristic of coastal areas is the frequent occurrence of local wind circulations called land and sea breezes. These are sporadic in mid-latitudes, but in the tropics they blow virtually every day. Both occur because land and water absorb and lose heat from the sun at different rates. During the day, the land heats far more quickly than the sea, and air begins to rise. As warm air rises above the land, cool air from the sea is drawn in underneath, creating a stiff sea breeze, blowing inland. At night, the situation is reversed. The land cools more quickly, and air begins to sink. The cool air pushes out under the warm air over the sea. This is called a land breeze.

Colours in the sky

PURE SUNLIGHT IS WHITE, but it is made up of the seven colours of the rainbow mixed together. As sunlight passes through the atmosphere, gases, dust, ice crystals, and water droplets in the air split it into its rich variety of colours. Clear skies look blue because gases in the air bounce mostly blue light towards our eyes. Sunset skies may be fiery red because the rays of the setting sun travel so far through the dense, lower atmosphere that nearly all but red is absorbed. But the endless stirring of the atmosphere by sun and wind constantly brings new colours to the sky. Sometimes, sunlight strikes ice and water in the air to create spectacular effects such as rainbows and triple suns. Rainbows form in showery weather, when there is a break in the clouds after rain, and always appear on the opposite side of the sky to the sun. Occasionally, electrical discharges can bring dramatic colour to the sky – particularly at night.

THE COLOURS OF THE MOON
On rare occasions, raindrops may catch the reflection of bright moonlight to form a moonbow. The colours of the moonbow are faint but they are the same as those seen in a rainbow during the daytime.

POLAR LIGHTS
Occasionally, highly charged particles from the sun strike gases in the atmosphere high above the poles to create a spectacular display of coloured lights in the night sky. In the northern hemisphere, this is known as the *aurora borealis*; in the southern hemisphere, it is known as the *aurora australis*.

WRAPPED IN A RAINBOW
Rainbows seem to appear and disappear so miraculously that many cultures believe they have magical properties. To the Navajo Indians of southwest USA the rainbow is a spirit. The spirit is depicted on this blanket around two other supernatural beings, with a sacred maize, or corn, plant in the centre.

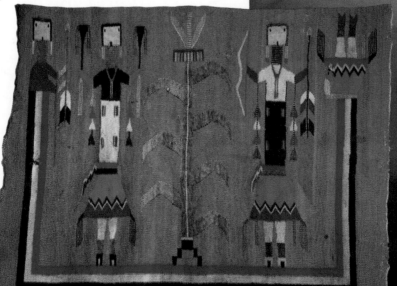

Low, stratus-type clouds in shadow

SAINTLY LIGHT
In thundery weather, sailors occasionally see a strange, glowing ball of light on the masthead. Called "St. Elmo's Fire", this is actually an electrical discharge, like lightning.

THREE SUNS AT ONCE
A colourful halo, or ring, around the sun is often seen in cirrostratus and, occasionally, high altostratus clouds. This phenomenon is caused by ice crystals in the cloud refracting, or bending, sunlight. Bright "mock suns", or sundogs, may also appear, with long, white tails pointing away from the left or right of the real sun.

MISTY GIANTS
The "Brocken Spectre" appears when sunlight projects the enlarged shadows of mountaineers onto low-lying mist or clouds nearby.

WATER COLOURS
Rainbows are sunlight that is bent and reflected by raindrops. As the light enters a raindrop it is bent slightly. It is reflected from the back of the drop and bent again as it leaves the front. It is the bending that separates the white light into its separate colours. Each drop splits light into all of the colours, but they leave the drop at different angles, so you see only one colour from a particular drop. The colours are always in the same order: red (on the outside of a primary bow), orange, yellow, green, blue, indigo, and violet.

Rainbow is created by reflection from rain in a cloud much higher in the sky

Receding cumulonimbus cloud

Red on the top or outside of a "primary" rainbow

Yellow in the rainbow's centre

Violet on the bottom or inside of the rainbow

From aeroplanes, a rainbow can sometimes be seen as a full circle

Home weather station

Professional meteorologists have a great deal of sophisticated equipment and thousands of weather stations to help them track the weather (pp. 12–13). But you can easily keep your own local weather watch with simple instruments – some of which can be made easily at home – and your own eyes. The longer the period over which observations are made, the more interesting and more valuable they become. But you must take measurements at exactly the same time at least once every day, without fail. This way your records can be more easily compared with those made by the professionals. The most important readings are rainfall, temperature range, wind speed and direction, and air pressure. If you can, record the humidity and soil temperature as well, and make a visual estimate of how much of the sky is covered by cloud.

HIGH WINDS
Professional meteorologists have always tried to mount instruments for measuring wind speeds on special masts or high buildings. Here the wind is least affected by obstructions on the ground.

Protractor

50 kph (30 mph)

25 kph (15 mph)   *10 kph (6 mph)*   *0 kph (0 mph)*

Cotton thread

Table-tennis ball

Home-made wind gauge, or "anemometer"

Ventimeter

Air pressure in millibars

Air pressure in pounds per square inch

Moving pointer indicating pressure

Pointer to indicate lowest pressure reached

An aneroid barometer has a face like a clock

WIND SPEED
You can roughly measure the wind speed using a table-tennis ball glued to the end of a thread that has been tied to the centre of a protractor (left). By holding the protractor parallel to the wind, you can read the angle the ball is blown to by the wind and so work out the wind speed. A hand-held, plastic ventimeter (right) is much more accurate, but more expensive.

AIR PRESSURE
A barometer (pp. 10–11) is perhaps the most useful instrument of all, if you want to make forecasts as well as keep records. It clearly shows a drop in pressure bringing storms, and a rise in pressure promising good weather. When a storm approaches, take a reading every 30 minutes to see how fast and how far the pressure falls. Unfortunately, even simple aneroid barometers like this are expensive.

A bead ensures that the vane rotates easily

N

Arrowhead shows the wind direction – that is, where it is blowing from

Dowel pole

WIND DIRECTION
A wind vane can be made with balsa wood and mounted on a dowel pole. Make the vane's head smaller than its tail (the pointer indicates where the wind is coming from). Paint it to protect from rain and use a compass to work out exactly where north and south are.

CLOUD SNAPS
Photographs provide an accurate visual record of unusual weather conditions. It is important to make a note of the exact time and date when the picture was taken, and write it on the processed print.

SOIL TEMPERATURE
Special, right-angled thermometers are used to measure the temperature beneath the surface of the ground. Plants will survive if frost does not penetrate very deeply.

TEMPERATURE RANGE
A double-ended thermometer records the maximum and minimum temperatures reached each day. A magnet is used to reset the indicators every time a reading is taken. It is important to mount the thermometer out of direct sunlight – preferably in a box painted white, mounted a metre or so above the ground, and drilled with large holes for good ventilation.

RAINFALL
A simple, plastic rain-gauge is quite accurate, provided you set it up securely at ground level in an exposed place. Each day take the measuring cylinder out to make a reading, empty it, and dry thoroughly. If you do not empty it, remember to subtract the previous day's measurement from your total each time.

Rain-gauge

HUMIDITY
A wet and dry hygrometer has two thermometers: the bulb of one is kept wet in distilled water and the other bulb dry. The difference in temperature between them indicates humidity on a scale provided by the makers. Only when the humidity is high can fog or clouds form.

WEATHER SKETCHES
Drawing clouds and other weather phenomena is a good way of learning to tell one type from another, and analyzing how they are formed.

SUN SCREENS
Professional weather instruments are kept inside ventilated shelters, known as Stevenson Screens. These protect them from direct sunlight, which could cause false results.

COME WIND OR RAIN ...
Weather records must be taken at the same time each day, even if it is raining hard.

Measuring cylinder

KEEPING RECORDS
Record all instrument readings, along with the date and time, in a proper notebook divided into appropriate columns. Do not use a loose-leaf book, as pages could be lost.

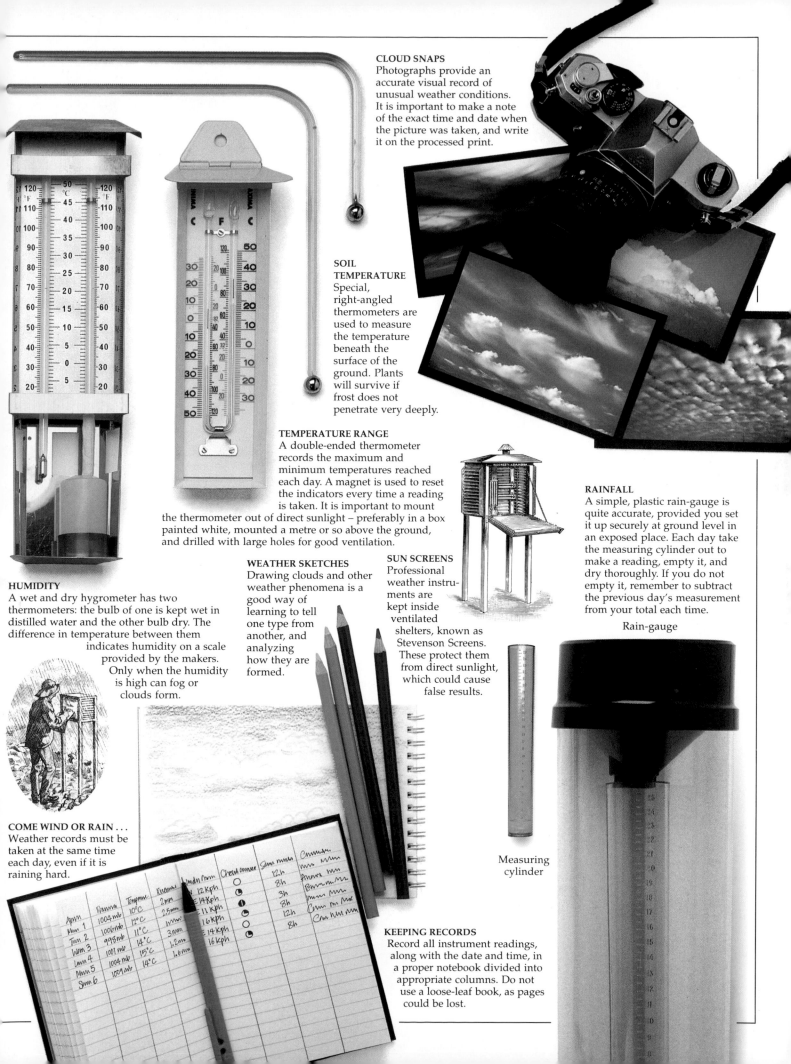

Did you know?

AMAZING FACTS

⚡ 12% of the Earth's surface is permanently covered in snow and ice, a total area of about 21 million sq. km (8 million sq. miles). 80% of the world's fresh water takes the form of snow or ice, mainly at the North and South Poles.

Frozen waterfall in the Zanskar Range Himalaya mountains, India

⚡ In very cold winters, waterfalls freeze over. Ice grows out from the side of a waterfall as splashed drops of water freeze, one on top of the other. Even the Niagara Falls in North America, one of the largest waterfalls in the world, freezes over.

⚡ The atmosphere contains 2.4 billion cubic km (1½ billion cubic miles) of air and about 15,470 trillion litres (34 trillion gallons) of water. Because of gravity, 80% of the air and nearly all the moisture are in the troposphere, the part of the atmosphere closest to Earth.

⚡ Sunbathing can be dangerous on sunny days when there are clouds in the sky. The clouds reflect so much ultraviolet light from the sun that they increase the amount of harmful ultraviolet rays that reach the ground, increasing the risk of skin cancer.

⚡ Very hot weather can kill. If it is too hot or humid for people's sweat to evaporate and cool them down, they get heatstroke. This can lead to collapse, coma, and even death.

⚡ The biggest desert in the world is Antarctica. It only has about 127 mm (5 in) of precipitation (snow or rain) a year, just a little more than the Sahara Desert.

⚡ It can snow in the desert! Snow sometimes falls during the winter in cold deserts, such as the Great Basin Desert in the USA and the Gobi Desert in Asia.

⚡ In 1939, hundreds of frogs, many of them still alive, fell from the sky during a storm in England. They had probably been sucked up from ponds and rivers by small tornadoes, then fell to the ground again with the rain.

Raining frog

⚡ A staggering 500 million litres (110 million gallons) of rain can fall from a single thunderstorm.

⚡ The average cloud only lasts for about ten minutes.

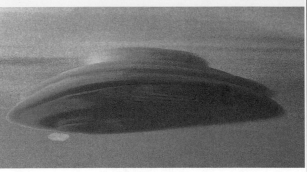

Lenticular cloud

⚡ Many reported sightings of UFOs have turned out to be lenticular (lens-shaped) clouds. Waves of wind blowing around mountaintops form smooth, rounded clouds like flying saucers which hover motionless for hours at a time.

⚡ Hailstones sometimes grow enormous. The largest authenticated hailstone in the world fell on Coffeyville, USA in 1970 and weighed 0.77 kg (1 lb 11 oz). An even bigger one is said to have fallen on Bangladesh in 1986.

⚡ Trees in forests around the world are being destroyed by acid rain. Acid rain forms when pollutants from factories and cars interact with sunlight and water vapour in the clouds to form sulphuric and nitric acids. These contaminate water supplies and damage forests and crops.

Conifers destroyed by acid rain

QUESTIONS AND ANSWERS

Q Why does the weather keep changing all the time?

A The heat of the sun keeps the lower atmosphere constantly moving. How much the sun heats the air varies across the world, throughout the day and through the year. These variations mean that the weather is constantly changing.

Q What makes the wind blow?

A Winds blow wherever there is a difference in air temperature and pressure. They always blow from an area of high pressure to an area of low pressure.

Solar corona

Q Why are there sometimes coloured rings around the sun?

A Fuzzy, coloured rings around the sun are called a solar corona. They appear when the sun is covered by a thin layer of cloud. The water droplets in the cloud split the sunlight, creating a rainbow effect.

Q What makes a large, bright disc around the moon ?

A A lunar corona occurs when sunlight reflected from the moon passes through the water droplets in thin cloud.

The Earth pillars of Hoodoos

Q How has the weather made desert rocks such strange shapes?

A Over time, desert rocks are worn away by the weather. Temperature changes and water make rocks crack and shatter. Also, windblown sand acts like sandpaper. It wears away softer rock, leaving strange shapes, such as pillars and arches.

Q Why are some deserts hot in the day and freezing cold at night?

A Above hot deserts, the skies are clear. The ground becomes baking hot by day because there are no clouds to shield it, but it turns cold at night because there is nothing to trap the heat, which is lost back into the atmosphere.

Q What is a mirage and where do they appear?

A Mirages are tricks of the light created by very hot air. Air close to the ground is much hotter than the air above it, and light bends as it passes from one temperature to the other. This creates a shimmering reflection that looks like water. Deserts are renowned for producing mirages that look like oases.

Desert mirage

Q How big do the biggest clouds grow?

A The biggest clouds are cumulonimbus, the big, dark rain clouds that often produce thunderstorms. They can be up to 9.7 km (6 miles) high and hold half a million tonnes of water.

Q Where is the best place to see the tops of clouds?

A Aeroplanes usually fly above the clouds, and mountain tops are also sometimes above the clouds.

Q How powerful is the average thunderstorm?

A A typical thunderstorm about 1 km (0.6 miles) across has about the same amount of energy as ten atom bombs.

Q When is the best time to see a rainbow?

A The best rainbows often appear in the morning or late afternoon, when the sun is out and rain is falling in the distance. Stand with your back to the sun and look towards the rain to see the rainbow. The lower the sun is in the sky, the wider the bow will be.

Record Breakers

❄ **THE COLDEST PLACE:**
The lowest temperture recorded in the world is -89.2°C (-128.6°F) at Vostok Station, Antarctica on 21st July 1983.

❄ **THE HOTTEST PLACE:**
At Al'Aziziyah, Libya, the temperature reached a record high of 58°C (136°F) on 13th September, 1922.

❄ **THE DRIEST PLACE:**
Arica in Chile's Atacama Desert is the driest recorded place on Earth, with less than 0.75 mm (0.03 in) of rain a year for 59 years.

❄ **THE WETTEST PLACE:**
Lloro, Colombia, is the rainiest place in the world, receiving an average 1,330 cm (525 in) of rain a year for 29 years.

❄ **THE FASTEST WINDS:**
The fastest winds on Earth are inside the funnel of a tornado. They spin at speeds of up to 480 km (300 miles) an hour.

Working with weather

La Rance tidal barrage, France

IN RECENT YEARS, scientists have become increasingly worried that human activities may be changing the climate. Meteorologists are constantly doing research into the weather, often in dangerous conditions, to make long-range predictions viable. To reduce emissions of pollutant gases, scientists are also harnessing the power of the weather to provide alternative, cleaner sources of energy.

TIDAL POWER

The energy of the tides can be harnessed by building a barrage across a suitable estuary. As the water flows in and out twice a day, it passes through turbines, which generate clean, renewable electricity. The biggest tidal energy plant in the world crosses the La Rance estuary in Brittany, France. It provides electricity for 25,000 households.

The aircraft are equipped with data-gathering instruments

The WC-130 normally carries a crew of six people

US Air Force WC-130 aircraft

TORNADO ALLEY

Tornados are more common in the United States than anywhere else. They strike regularly in an area known as Tornado Alley, made up of the states between South Dakota and Texas.

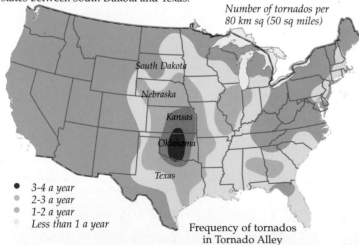

Number of tornados per 80 km sq (50 sq miles)

South Dakota

Nebraska

Kansas

Oklahoma

Texas

- 3-4 a year
- 2-3 a year
- 1-2 a year
- Less than 1 a year

Frequency of tornados in Tornado Alley

HURRICANE HUNTERS

In the USA, an Air Force squadron, known as the Hurricane Hunters, flies aircraft through hurricanes to monitor them and predict when and where they will hit land. The specially adapted aircraft fly through a hurricane in an X pattern, passing through the eye every two hours, and transmit information by satellite to the National Hurricane Center. The air crews can detect dangerous changes in a hurricane's intensity and movement that are hard to predict by satellite alone.

Prairie tornado photograph taken by a storm chaser

STORM CHASERS

Some scientists risk their lives by studying tornadoes at close hand. These storm chasers carry out research, using Doppler radar dishes that enable them to look right inside storm clouds to see signs of a developing tornado. Their research helps forecasters to give advance warning of danger.

GENERAL WEATHER WEBSITES

- The BBC website is an excellent starting point for finding out about weather; it also provides links to other good websites. Visit it at:
  www.bbc.co.uk/weather
- The Met Office's award-winning website is at:
  www.metoffice.com
- This Australian site also has lots of useful information:
  www.bom.gov.au

LIFE IN THE FREEZER
Meteorologists and other scientists based at various research stations in Antarctica carry out detailed research into changing climate conditions. They also monitor the seasonal hole in the ozone layer that lies above Antarctica to find out how pollution and our efforts to prevent it are affecting the atmosphere.

Scientist launching a weather balloon into the atmosphere

Meteorologist servicing an automatic weather station

SOLAR POWER
The Sun is potentially the most powerful source of renewable energy. Solar power stations aim to capture this energy by using thousands of wide mirrors to collect and concentrate as much sunlight as possible. Luz, in the Mojave Desert, in California, USA, has the biggest solar power station in the world. 650,000 enormous solar mirrors reflect heat onto tubes filled with oil. The hot oil heats water, which in turn makes steam. This drives turbines that generate electricity.

ANTARCTIC RESEARCH
In Antarctica, meteorologists carry out experiments to improve the quality of weather forecasts and to make long-term predictions about climate change. Other scientists study the ice sheet for valuable information about climate changes in the past and the effects of current global warming. Oceanographers, geologists and biologists research the changing ocean conditions in the icy seas around Antarctica and their effects on plant and animal life.

Each of these mirrors is computer-controlled to track the Sun across the sky during the day

Wind farm near Palm Springs, California

CATCHING THE WIND
At wind farms, windmills convert the wind's energy into electricity. The windmills have to be far enough apart not to steal wind from each other. Wind farms only work in exposed places, and it takes about 3,000 windmills to generate as much power as a coal power station.

Find out more

- You can find out about hurricane hunters at: **www.hurricanehunters.com**
- For information on storm chasers, visit: **www.stormchaser.niu.edu**
- There is a lot of information about research in Antarctica on the website of the British Antarctic Survey: **www.bas.ac.uk**
- Find out about alternative technology at: **www.cat.org.uk**
- Alternatively, you could visit a specialized centre to see working examples of wind, water and solar power in action and to learn more about alternative energy sources.
One such centre is:
CENTRE FOR ALTERNATIVE TECHNOLOGY, MACHYNLLETH, POWYS, WALES SY20 9AZ

Extreme weather

WEATHER CAN BE VIOLENT and cause extensive damage. Every year, devastating floods, savage storms, blizzards, and prolonged periods of drought occur in different parts of the world, causing renewed speculation about climate change.

STORMS AND FLOODS

FLOODS
Floods cause more damage than any other natural phenomenon. They turn vast areas of dry land into massive lakes, destroying crops and making thousands of people homeless. In February 2000, freak rain in southern Africa caused the worst floods for 50 years in Mozambique. More than a million people had to leave their homes. Before the waters had receded, a cyclone hit the country, making the situation even worse.

Floods at Fenton, Missouri, USA

Flood victims wait to be airlifted from rooftops near Chokwe, Mozambique

HURRICANES
Katrina, a Category-5 hurricane that formed over the Atlantic in late 2005, caused incredible devastation when it struck the Gulf Coast of the USA, especially to New Orleans and other parts of Louisiana. Katrina brought ferocious winds, torrential rain, and gigantic tidal surges. It caused the deaths of around 1,800 people, making it one of the deadliest hurricanes ever in the history of the USA.

Damage from Hurricane Katrina

THE DUST BOWL
In a dust storm, towering walls of choking dust reach right up to the sky and blot out the sun, creating a ghostly yellow light. In the 1930s, the North American Midwest had no rain for five years, and thousands of hectares of fertile prairie grasslands were transformed into a desert known as the Dust Bowl. Hot winds tore across the land, causing suffocating dust storms, and about 5,000 people died as a result of heatstroke and breathing problems.

FIRE, SNOW AND LANDSLIDES

The eruption of Mount St Helens, USA

VOLCANIC WEATHER

Large volcanic eruptions affect the weather worldwide. When Mount St Helens, USA, erupted in Spring 1980, the entire top of the mountain was blown off. Ash from the volcano was carried by high winds right around the planet, leading to hazy skies, amazing sunsets and a brief drop in temperature. The eruption of Mount Pinatabu in 1999 caused a drop in temperature of 0.5°C (0.9°F) around the world.

WILDFIRE

Raging forest fires are often ignited when lightning strikes vegetation that has been parched by hot, dry weather. Australia has about 15,000 bush fires a year, but on 16 February 1983, now known as Ash Wednesday, a searing heatwave triggered hundreds of fires in different places all at the same time. Driven by strong winds, the fires spread at terrifying speed, engulfing a town, killing 70 people, and damaging thousands of hectares of land.

AVALANCHES

When heavy snow builds up on a steep slope, even a small vibration can trigger an avalanche. In winter 1999, the European Alps had mild weather followed by record snowfalls and strong winds. In Austria, a block of snow weighing 170,000 tonnes (187,000 tons) broke away from a mountain and crashed down to the village of Galtür below, killing more than 30 people.

Rescuers using poles to search for victims of the Austrian avalanche

Avalanche on Mount McKinley, Alaska

MUDSLIDES

Every five to seven years, a change in the wind drives an ocean current called El Niño towards the coast of South America, causing violent storms and torrential rain in some areas and drought in others. In December 1999, 10,000 people were killed in Venezuela by floods and huge mudslides. Torrential rain soaked into the hillsides causing the mudslides, which destroyed all buildings, roads and trees in their path.

Mudslides at La Guaira, Venezuela

Glossary

AIR MASS A large body of air covering much of a continent or ocean in which the temperature, surface pressure, and humidity are fairly constant.

AIR PRESSURE The force of air pressing down on the ground or any other horizontal surface. It is sometimes also called atmospheric pressure.

ANEMOMETER An instrument for measuring the speed of the wind.

ANTICYCLONE Also known as a "high", this is a body of air in which the air pressure is higher than it is in the surrounding air.

ATMOSPHERE The layer of gases surrounding the Earth, stretching about 1,000 km (600 miles) into space. All weather takes place in the lowest layer.

AURORA Bands of coloured light that appear in the night sky. In the northern hemisphere this phenomenon is called the northern lights or the aurora borealis; in the southern hemisphere, it is called the aurora australis.

Anemometer

BAROGRAPH An instrument that provides a continuous record of air pressure on a strip of paper wound around a revolving drum.

Barograph

BAROMETER An instrument for measuring air pressure. The most accurate type is the mercury barometer, which measures the distance pressure forces mercury up a glass tube containing a vacuum.

BLIZZARD A wind storm in which snow is blown into the air by strong winds at speeds of at least 56 kph (35 mph), reducing visibility to less than 400 m (¼ mile).

CIRRUS Feathery cloud that forms at high altitudes, where the air is very cold.

CLIMATE The normal pattern of weather conditions in a particular place or region, averaged over a long period of time.

CLOUDS Masses of condensed water vapour and ice particles floating in the sky. Ten types of cloud have been categorized, all based on three basic cloud forms: cumulus, stratus, and cirrus.

COLD FRONT The boundary line between warm and cold air masses with the cold air moving towards the area of warm air in front of it.

CONDENSATION The change from a gas, such as water vapour, to a liquid, such as water.

CONVECTION The transfer of heat by the vertical movement of air or water. It makes warm air rise.

CORIOLIS EFFECT The effect caused by the Earth's spinning, which makes winds and currents follow a curved path across the Earth's surface.

CUMULONIMBUS The type of cloud that produces heavy showers, thunderstorms, and tornadoes. It is bigger and darker than cumulus.

CUMULUS Large, fluffy clouds with flat bases and rounded tops often seen in sunny weather. They often mass together.

CYCLONE Also known as a "low", this is a body of air in which the air pressure is lower than it is in the surrounding air. It is also the name used to describe a hurricane in the Indian Ocean and Western Pacific.

DEPRESSION A weather system where there is a centre with low pressure. It is also sometimes known as a cyclone.

DEW Moisture in the air that has condensed on objects at or near the Earth's surface.

DEW POINT The temperature at which water vapour in the air will condense.

DRIZZLE Light rain made of drops that are smaller than 0.5 mm (0.02 in) across.

FOG Water that has condensed from water vapour into tiny droplets near the ground, reducing visibility to less than 1,000 m (1,100 yd).

FRONT The boundary between two air masses with different basic characteristics.

FROST White ice crystals that form on cold surfaces when moisture from the air freezes.

GALE A very strong wind that blows at speeds of 52-102 kph (32-63 mph).

GLOBAL WARMING A long-term increase in the temperature of the atmosphere, possibly caused by the greenhouse effect.

GREENHOUSE EFFECT The warming up of the Earth's surface, caused by radiation from the sun being trapped by gases in the lower atmosphere, just as heat is trapped in a greenhouse by the glass roof.

GUST A sudden temporary increase in wind speed.

HAIL Rounded drops of ice that fall from clouds.

HEMISPHERE Half of the Earth. There are northern and southern hemispheres.

HOAR FROST Spikes of frost that form when the air is about 0°C (32°F) and water vapour touches the surfaces of trees.

Hygrometer

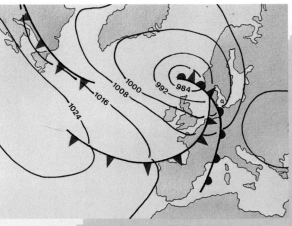
Weather chart showing fronts and isobars

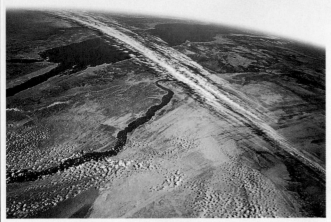
Jet stream clouds

METEOROLOGY The scientific study of weather, both in the atmosphere and at the surface of the Earth.

MILLIBAR The unit that is usually used by meteorologists when measuring and reporting atmospheric pressure.

MONSOON The seasonal shift in wind direction that makes wet seasons alternate with very dry seasons in India and Southeast Asia.

HUMIDITY The amount of water vapour that is in the air.

HURRICANE A tropical cyclone that occurs in the Caribbean and North Atlantic with winds of over 121 kph (75 mph) blowing around a centre of air at very low pressure.

HYGROMETER An instrument used for measuring humidity.

ISOBAR A line on a weather map that joins places with the same air pressure.

JET STREAM A band of very strong winds in the upper atmosphere, occasionally blowing at over 320 kph (200 mph).

LIGHTNING A visible discharge of static electricity from a cloud. Sheet lightning is a flash within a cloud. Fork lightning is a flash between a cloud and the ground.

OCCLUDED FRONT A front, or boundary, where cold air undercuts warm air, lifting it clear of the ground.

OZONE LAYER A thin layer of ozone gas in the upper atmosphere that filters out harmful ultraviolet radiation from the Sun before it reaches the Earth.

PRECIPITATION All forms of water that fall to the ground or form on or near it, such as rain, snow, dew and fog.

PREVAILING WIND The main direction from which the wind blows in a particular place.

RADIATION A process by which energy travels across space as electromagnetic waves, such as light and heat.

RADIOSONDE An instrument package that is sent into the upper atmosphere attached to a weather balloon. It radios weather information back to a receiving station on the ground.

RAIN GAUGE An instrument that is used to collect and measure the amount of rainfall.

RAIN SHADOW An area of decreased rainfall on the lee, or sheltered, side of a hill or mountain.

RIDGE An elongated area of high air pressure.

SMOG Originally, fog mixed with smoke, but now more commonly a haze that forms in polluted air in strong sunshine.

SNOW Ice crystals that fall from clouds in cold weather and which may stick together to form snowflakes.

STORM Strong winds, between gale and hurricane force, of 103-121 kph (64-75 mph), which uproot trees and overturn cars.

STRATOSPHERE The layer of the Earth's atmosphere above the troposphere.

STRATUS A vast, dull type of low-level cloud that forms in layers.

SUNSHINE RECORDER An instrument used to record the number of hours of sunshine in a day.

SYNOPTIC CHART A weather chart that provides detailed information about weather conditions at a particular time over a large area.

THERMAL A rising current of warm air.

THERMOSPHERE The top layer of the atmosphere, above about 90 km (56 miles).

THUNDER The sound made by expanding air during a flash of lightning.

THUNDERSTORM A rainstorm with thunder and lightning.

Sunshine recorder

TORNADO A narrow spiral of air rotating at high speed around an area of extremely low air pressure. Wind speeds may be higher than 320 kph (200 mph).

TROPOSPHERE The innermost layer of the Earth's atmosphere, where most of the weather takes place.

TROUGH An elongated area of low pressure.

TYPHOON A tropical cyclone that occurs over the Pacific Ocean.

WARM FRONT A boundary line between two air masses where the air behind the front is warmer than the air ahead of it.

WATERSPOUT A column of rapidly spiralling air that forms over warm and usually shallow water, or when a tornado crosses water.

WIND CHILL The sensation that the air temperature is lower than it really is because of the effect of the wind.

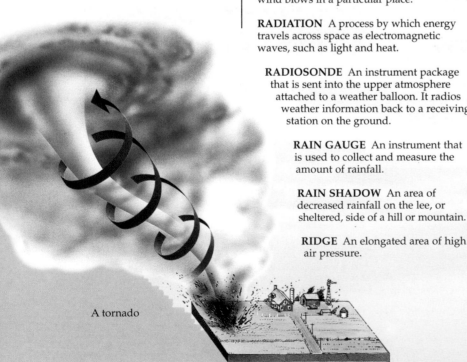
A tornado

Index

Acknowledgements

Dorling Kindersley would like to thank:
Robert Baldwin of the National Maritime Museum, Greenwich, for making instruments available for photography; The Meteorological Office, Bracknell, for providing instruments for photography; Met Check for the loan of instruments on pp. 62–63; David Donkin for weather models on pp. 26, 34–33, 34–35, 44–45, and 53; Sophie Mitchell for her help in the initial stages of the book; and Jane Parker for the index.

For this edition, the publisher would also like to thank: Lisa Burke for assisting with revisions; Claire Bowers, David Ekholm–JAlbum, Sunita Gahir, Joanne Little, Nigel Ritchie, Susan St Louis, Carey Scott, and Bulent Yusef for the clipart; David Ball, Neville Graham, Rose Horridge, Joanne Little, and Sue Nicholson for the wallchart.

The publisher would like to thank the following for their kind permission to reproduce their images:

Picture credits
a-above; b-below; c-centre; f-far; l-left; r-right; t=top; m=middle
Alison Anholt-White: 19, 28bc, 42cr. **Aviation Picture Library:** 20cl. **Bridgeman Art Library:** 17t, 42tl, 42bl, 43tr, 43br. **British Antarctic Survey:** 60c. **Bruce Coleman Picture Library:** 8cl, 14cr, 20c, 28tr, 28–29c, 29tl, 52b, 54bl, 54–55, 59tc. **Corbis:** Tony Arruza 68bl; Bettmann 68tr; Gary Braasch 69tl; John H. Clark 66c; Philip James Corwin 67bl; Graham Neden; Ecoscene 67tl, 67tr; Jim Richardson 68br; Kevin Schafer 67cb. **B. Cosgrove:** 24–25, 24c, 24cr, 24bl, 25tr, 25cl, 28cl, 28c, 29tr, 29ctr, 29cr, 29cbr, 29br, Benjamin Lowy 68bl. **Daily Telegraph Colour Library:** 7tr, 43tc. **Dr. E. K. Degginger:** 46cl, 46cr, 47tr, 47c, 47b. **E. T. Archive:** 12c, 21br, 31br, 36tr. **European Space Agency:** 13tr. **Mary Evans Picture Library:** 10bc, 13bl, 20tl, 24tr, 30tl, 30bl, 37tr, 41br, 44tl, 45br, 46bl, 47l, 48b, 53cr, 54cl, 60cl, 60cr. **Courtesy of FAAM:** BAE Systems Regional Aircraft 12-13ca; With thanks to Maureen Smith and the Met Office UK. Photo by Doug Anderson 13cr. **Werner Forman**

Archive: 18cl, 36bl, 38c, 58b, 61tl. **Courtesy of Kate Fox:** 22b. **Hulton Deutsch Collection:** 55br. **Hutchison Library:** 31bl, 61bl. **Image Bank/ Getty Images:** 43cr, 56–57, 57tr, 66br. **Istituto e Museo di Storia della Scienza (photos Franca Principe):** 2br, 3bl, 10bl, 10r, 11tl, 11c, 11r, 11b. **Landscape Only:** 23cr. **Frank Lane Picture Library:** 20bl, 22tl, 30c, 36c, 41bl, 44bl. **Mansell Collection:** 18tl, 43cbl, 43cl. **Meteorological Office:** 12bl, 12br © Crown, 14cl, 15tl, 21t, 34t, 42tr, 45tl, 45tcl, 45c, 45tcr, 45tr, 49bl. **N.A.S.A.:** 16tl. **National Centre for Atmospheric Research:** 13br, 37tc. **N.H.P.A.:** 44cl. **R.K.Pilsbury:** 8crt, 8crb, 15tc, 26–27, 32cl, 33tl, 33c, 34cl, 34bl, 35t, 50cl, 50c, 50cr, 51tc, 51tl, 51br. **Planet Earth:** 9cl, 18cr, 20br, 23cl, 41t, 53tr, 54br, 55bl, 56b. **Popperfoto:** 21bl, Peter Andrews/ Reuters 68cl; Andy Mettler/Reuters 69cr; Kimberly White/Reuters 69br. **Rex Features:** 13tl. **Ann Ronan Picture Library:** 6tl, 12t, 13cl, 14tl, 23bl, 27bl, 27br, 38tl, 61cr. **Royal Meteorological Society:** 28tl. David Sands: 25br. **M. Saunders:** 20–21t. **Scala:** 11tc. **Science Photo Library:** 36-37,

40c, 40bl, 40bc, 58c, 58–59, 61cl; Simon Fraser 64cl, 64br; Damien Lovegrove 65bl; Magrath/Folsom 64tr; David Nunuk 65tc; Pekka Parviainen 65cl. Frank Spooner/Gamma: 38bl. **Stock Boston:** 48c. **Tony Stone Picture Library:** 6bl, 18bl, 31t, 48–49, 52–53. **Wildlife Matters:** 8tr, 9tr. **Zefa:** 7cb, 7b, 24cl, 25tl, 39t, 47tc, 49br, 50bl, 61br.

Illustrations by: Eugene Fleury, John Woodcock

Wallchart:
Alamy Images: Michael Freeman br; **BAE Systems Regional Aircraft:** fcl (Aircraft); **Corbis:** crb; Lynsey Addario bl; Roger Ressmeyer cr (Lightning); **FAAM / Doug Anderson, Maureen Smith & Met Office, UK:** cl; **Science Photo Library:** NOAA cl (Storm)

All other images © Dorling Kindersley. For further information see: **www.dkimages.com**